MISSION POSSIBLE:
Winning the Battle Over
TEMPTATION
Helping Individuals, Families and Organizations

MISSION POSSIBLE:
Winning the Battle Over
TEMPTATION
Helping Individuals, Families and Organizations

Gil Stieglitz

Unless otherwise noted, all Scriptures are taken from the New American Standard Bible, C 1960,1963,1968,1971,1972,1973,19 75,1977 by The Lockman Foundation, Used by permission.

ISBN 978-1-59684-289-2

Printed by Pathway Press, Cleveland, TN

DEDICATION

This book is dedicated to
Colonel Richard Hum USAF
*who years ago as my Youth Pastor
taught me to apply Scripture to any problem
I faced including temptation.*

*This book is also dedicated to
those brave men and women who are willing to:*

"strive against sin to the point of the shedding of blood,"

"fight the good fight of faith," and

"flee from youthful lust."

In a recovery group start with Section 1 If you are going to be teaching start with Section 2 then do Section

CONTENTS

PREFACE

Every book is a team effort of writing, refining, editing, rewriting and interaction. I appreciate so much all the people who have helped put this book together. My prayer is that this book will be a battle manual in the hands of many so that the power of the Scriptures will be released in their lives.

I need to express my thanks to my wife and beautiful girls for the time they allowed me to have to write this book. Our desire together is that men and women would move on to a new level of purity because of the prayer, work and encouragement of this book.

Let me also thank the students and graduates at Western Seminary Sacramento Extension for their help in refining the manuscript: Kyle Hedwall, Dawson Lange, Josh Remy, Randall Broadhurst, and Gabe Garcia.

I also must thank four of the pastors at Adventure Church in Roseville, California, who were willing to read and work through this manuscript and add invaluable insights and comments: Pastors Dave Doty, Bill Corbin, Ryan Haynes and John Moton.

INTRODUCTION

She deposited her husband in my office screaming through clenched teeth, "**FIX HIM!**" In her opinion their marriage was over. His problem was acting on destructive desires. As he lay sleeping at night he would talk in his sleep about the women he was having affairs with at his office. This was more than his wife could take. She threw him into my office as a last resort. Her husband seemed like any mild-mannered, hard-working husband. He went to work and came home to his family. What I did not know, until later, was that he had struggled with pornography since he was a small boy, and marital infidelity for the last 10 years. His wife brought him to me at this point because she had reached a breaking point. I was either going to fix this sexual addiction he had or she was done. I began working with him using the principles that I will describe in this book. I have found that actually doing exercises and projects based upon Scriptural verses and concepts has a profound impact on freeing people from the grip of lust. After listening and interacting with this somewhat guilt-ridden husband, I began the process of assigning practical spiritual exercises based upon Scripture to break him free from his almost life long captivity to lust. The transformation over the next 6 months was almost unbelievable. The roots of his addiction to sensuality and immorality had spread to almost all aspects of his life, and when he was freed from lust's grip it was like he was a new man. He said to me, "As long as I meditate on Scripture and keep up the exercises you have given me, I don't feel the pull of those old impulses." His wife was very ecstatic because of the "new" man in her home. He was attentive to her and to the children in ways that he never had been before. He found new enjoyment in the relationships with his family and friends. He was no longer constantly pursuing the big thrill—sex. Most men do not understand how their selfish pursuit of lust deeply damages the real joy that is possible in their marriage and family. The more lust captures your heart the less you will be able to respond in kindness, sensitivity and wise counsel to your sons and daughters, your spouse, your co-workers and your friends. The more obsessed with lust you become the less you will be able to build the kind of marriage that can satisfy you at the deep level that you need. It is absolutely essential that people learn how to break free from lust and move into the land of purity.

Lust is a powerful foe. It comes at us from both the inside and the outside. On the inside, it is one form of selfishness that seeks to corrupt us, to direct us and to possess us. On the inside, lust seeks to use your own natural physiology against you, demanding that you release the growing sexual interest whenever and wherever you want. On the outside, in this culture, it uses clothing styles, words, attitudes, stories, jokes, the media and provocative actions to lure you into making it the number one pursuit of your life. Make no mistake lust does seeks to dominate you.

Now let's make an important distinction between sex and lust. Sex is an extremely pleasurable gift that God gave to mankind to bond a husband and wife together, to create a family, to draw men away from work to home, and to open up a man and a woman to levels of intimacy that would not be as easy without it. Lust however, seeks to rip that gift of intimacy and openness out of its only approved container (marriage) and allow you to get high on the pleasure with none of the responsibility. Lust narrows the promise of sexual intimacy down to physical erotic pleasure. It makes physical intimacy taking rather than giving. Lust is unlicensed selfishness and desire. It is a beast that lives within all of us. Not everyone is captured by this particular selfish beast, some are captured by greed or envy or pride, but many are completely captured by selfish desire for erotic pleasure, and it redirects the course of their lives. If a young man does not learn how to handle the lustful impulses that rise up from within him and assault him from without, it will diminish his potential, connect him to the wrong people, introduce him to choices he never should have seen, and inject disease, guilt and shame into his life. If you allow yourself to be captured by this beast you will always be chasing and never really know intimacy. It promises a short cut to true soul connection and yet it cannot deliver. Your soul will remain parched for real connection, even as your body is used up and damaged.

What Are Destructive Desires?

We live in a day and age when almost all desires are considered normal. It is only after the destruction that some desires are seen as wrong. And in some cases our culture is unwilling to trace the problem back to the desire itself. Our culture wants to pretend that it is only the judgmental actions of the society that condemns certain desires. Our culture wants to pretend that the desire itself is not what brings the destruction. In spite of what our culture is saying, there are destructive desires that will destroy you, destroy your relationships, and destroy your potential. We have to go back to God's blueprint for mankind to clearly grasp what desires are good and right, and which ones are destructive and wicked.

The Scripture uses the word *epithumia* for destructive desire. It is a Greek word that means any strong, overwhelming, or uncontrolled desire. The church for thousands of years has used the word lust to describe what this word meant. It is an overwhelming desire to get what you want, to satisfy something that would pleasure you. There are all kinds of these desires. These overwhelming, uncontrollable, and selfish desires are destructive. They will, if embraced and expressed, bring about damage, chaos and destruction.

Destructive desires go outside of the boundaries of true love. Destructive desires are selfish desires. Scripture lists three categories of destructive desires from least to greatest: Sensuality to Adultery to Perversion. The goal of destructive desires is to get you to live your life on a selfish plane. Thinking about yourself and what you want and how you can get pleasure, rather than how you can really meet the needs of others, and be in encouraging relationships with others.

What Happens if We Give in to Destructive Desires?

The answer to this question has largely been ignored in our day. Our culture wants to ignore that there are reasons why people in the past obeyed God's laws. They wanted to be healthy in their spirit, in their mind, in their emotions, in their will, in their body. When we give into selfish sexual desires we will become more selfish, we will begin to harm others as we pursue our desires, we will pick up diseases, we will increase our loneliness, we will suffer emotional trauma, we will experience emotional trauma, we will have pains of guilt and spiritual separation. These and many other kinds of difficulties are unleashed when we give into lust and sexual temptation.

It is absolutely crucial that people, especially young people, learn how to say "No" to the sexual and sensual impulses that bubble up from within them. Our society is full of ways to try to get young people to try and let these lustful promptings poke to the surface and express themselves. It is like the barkers at a cheesy carnival yelling at you to come and waste your money. In this case the wasting is your youth, your innocence, your potential and your kindness.

WINNING THE BATTLE OVER TEMPTATION is not about saying **NO** to temptation in more effective ways. It is about being free from the domination of lust. Jesus said, **"Blessed are the pure in heart for theirs is the kingdom of heaven."** There is a place where you can perceive God and care for others without the constant pressure from lust. The material that will be shared in this book is designed to get you to that spiritual place where your perception of God is greater and your enjoyment of truly loving others reaches another level. The deeper that you descend into lust, and it is a deep hole, the less perceptive you will be of God's presence.

Most Christian men do not expect that they will win the war against impure thoughts, but it is possible. God has called us to take each thought captive and take it to Christ for evaluation (2 Cor. 10:3-5). If we believe defeat is inevitable then this will be a self-fulfilling prophecy. If we believe that even when we win one battle there is always another more powerful temptation coming behind it, then we will not put up much resistance to the impulses to lust. God want us realize that victory is possible, and to be determined and commit ourselves to winning this war with lust and living in a mentally pure and wholesome place.

Yes, we may lose a battle now and again, but if we are committed to winning the war against impure thoughts, God will turn every defeat into a new learning experience. We must not try to just cut down on the number of times that we entertain impure thoughts, but instead we must push toward a place where love and benefit and righteousness for others is possible instead of the selfishness of lust being our dominant thought. We must resist the impulses to sexual selfishness as the book of Hebrews exhorts all of us to do, "You have not yet resisted to the point of the shedding of blood in your striving against sin." (Heb. 12:4)

When we are in a battle with lust we lose focus and clarity on the important issues in our lives. In fact God suggests that when we face the temptation to lust we will either turn away and see the Lord clearly or we will embrace our strong desire for sexual gratification and stop perceiving the Lord (Matt. 5:8). How tragic to trade a clear, vibrant perception of God for a few moments of sensual pleasure. Realize that you cannot be in love with the lusts of this world and be vibrantly in love with the Father. These elements are mutually exclusive (1 John 2:15-18).

It is crucial that we remain perceptive to the presence and guidance of the Lord Jesus Christ, especially when we are facing strong temptation to lust. Lust, like carbon monoxide attaching to our red blood cells, makes a quicker connection to our soul and shuts out our ability to perceive the presence of God and His guidance. We need to say NO to lust and YES to God. (Matt. 5:8; James 4:7-10; 1 Pet. 5:6-10; Jer. 29:11-14)

This book will detail three simple steps that when applied consistently will deliver a person from the cesspool of lust and immorality. God has invested His word with power to change lives and when we do what it says, it does set us free. It is not enough to know what to do, but not do it. I grow weary of people who want to hear some new truth and have the hearing of it set them free. It is not hearers of the Word that enjoy new levels of spiritual growth and joy, but it is doers of the Word (James 1:22). These three simple steps will only help a person if they do them. Jesus castigates those who heard Him, **"Why do you call me Lord, Lord, but do not do what I say?"** (Luke 6:46) Doing the assignments in this book usually requires a spiritual director or small group who will make the assignments, check the homework, and watch people demonstrate that they understand how to live out the new skills. The three steps are simple but they will not be easy. They will require focus, dedication and new routines in your life. What are the three steps: *First,* cleansing from your past sexual sins; *Second,* strengthening your defenses against the seduction and attacks of temptation; ***Third,*** closing spiritual, emotional, psychological doorways that increase lust's power.

Before we begin to explore the specific steps and exercises let me encourage you that it is possible to get a handle on lust and live a life of purity. Listen to what others have said after beginning to practice the exercises and projects that are listed in this chapter.

"I would not have believed it, if it wasn't happening to me. I am free from lust in a way that in my mind was impossible." Businessman

"The sexual quiet in my mind is amazing. I can think about other things without every 3 seconds having a sexual thought crowding into my mind." Student

"I can go to a public place without fighting the images in my head. I don't have to undress all the women I see anymore." Ex convict

"I did not believe that this mental place was possible." Soldier

"I am not thinking about sex all the time." Student

"Mentally I am clearer than I have ever been." Graduate student

Successfully battling lust is possible but requires constant vigilance and practicing the spiritual exercises that grow out of the Scriptures. Just as an athlete must keep training in order to maintain their performance, so freedom from lust requires a level of spiritual formation that is not automatic or typical. Allowing yourself to get out of shape either physically or spiritually means making the easy choice and being unwilling to train and practice. Training for a life of love instead of lust is worth it.

HOW TO USE THIS BOOK

This book was written so that men and women would begin doing real Biblical Exercises that would empower them to win in the Battle with Lust. Therefore if the exercises are not attempted, this book will be of little value to you.

Personal Study

This book can be a personal study. If you are working through this book alone, then take each chapter and do at least one of the exercises in that chapter. Mark any exercises that are especially helpful in pushing back the power of lust in your life. Some exercises need to be practiced for a week before their effectiveness can be displayed. If you find one exercise that is not helpful, then simply move on to the next exercise. Do not be in hurry to get through the book. Let the power of the Biblical exercises get through you. If you find that one exercise is particularly helpful then stay with that one exercise for a month or longer, in fact, that effective exercise may become the backbone of your winning strategy for battling lust. If you want to add others to this one that is particularly powerful, then keep going through the book and adding more. But it is more important that you discover how to win in this battle against lust than that you finish the book in a certain time frame. This book may take you a year or longer to go through. Keep doing at least one new exercise per week until you have gone through the material at least once. You should be in a different place at the end of that cycle. You may then want to get into a group study in which you go through the material with others.

Mentor-Directed Study

This book can be done as a mentor-directed study. This is where a well-respected, Godly leader takes you through this material and evaluates your progress. Each week or month the mentor will assign chapters and exercises. The next time you gather together, significant amounts of time should be given to describing what happened when you did the exercises. If they were not done or were not done well, then the same exercises should be repeated. It is crucial to not be in a hurry to get through this material. It is far more important that the Biblical material make a lasting change and impact. In my opinion the mentor-directed study is the most powerful and effective way of deploying this type of soul-stretching material. One of the most effective ways I have seen a mentor-directed study get started is for the person with the desire for a mentor-directed study to ask a person that they highly respect to mentor them over this material. The mentor is asked if they would be willing to meet with the individual or small group and walk them through the material.

A second way that a mentor-directed study can be initiated is by the mentor. He/she can pray and ask the Lord to direct them to those who might be ready for a deeper spiritual growth study like this one. Either by phone or in person, ask people God has put on your heart if they would be interested in growing deeper through a weekly study of this type. If they say yes, then sign them up and put them in a small group of people like them. If they say no, then that is okay—they are just not ready.

Class or Lecture Series

This book can be covered as a Bible Study Class, Adult Sunday School Class, or a Men's Ministry Class. If there is less than 6 people in the class I would recommend that you adopt the Mentor format rather than the Class style. But if there are 7 or more, then the lecture style can work quiet well. This study or one like it should be a constantly-repeating part of every Men's ministry in the country. If you would like to use the prepared presentation slides that go along with this book, you can go to the Principles to Live By website (*www.ptlb.com*) and download the power point slides. Please feel free to use these slides in the class. The best class format divides an hour and a half into three approximately equal segments of about 30 minutes. Start with prayer and about 20-30 minutes of sharing in small groups of 3-4 people of the same gender (this material is of such a nature that same-gender groups usually work out best) about how the exercises went from the last week. If there is widespread misunderstanding on the exercises that were taught the last time, then they should be explained again. Next, there should be 20-30 minute lecture on the next set of exercises. It may be appropriate to cover a few chapters rather than only one. Sometimes the information and/or exercises are so crucial that complete focus must be on a very limited amount of material. Remember that the goal is not to have people impressed with the teacher; the goal is to break them free from the grip of lust. That will only take place if they are actually doing the exercises. Finally, a class or study of 20-30 minutes should be set aside for actually doing the exercise in class. Have the people in the class actually try out the exercises. Then have the class commit to doing particular exercises during the week.

I would strongly suggest that the material in this book, or material like this, be set up to be a constantly-running class or support group in every church. Because every man faces this battle with sexual temptation constantly, I would recommend a gifted teacher(s) with a shepherd's heart be assigned to teach this class from beginning to end, covering no more than 3 exercises a week. Remember the goal is demonstrated skill in applying Biblical weapons against temptation. If a project or spiritual exercise needs to be repeated, then repeat it. When the class is over take a few weeks or a month off and then start teaching the class again. If your church is larger, start a new class every month or two so that new men in the church can start on the road to resistance and freedom. Do not believe that there needs to be a big attendance for this class. In fact it is almost better if the class is limited to no more than 12 at a time, as this will force men to get to know each other's name, and care for one another at a deeper level. Encourage men who have been through this material to go through the class as a refresher every 3 years or so. If a man is continuing to struggle in this area, even after they have taken the class once, then have them sign up to get into the next group that will be starting in the next few weeks. They need to apply the spiritual exercises more thoroughly to their lives. Sometimes a person needs the ongoing support of a group to help them stay free from the temptation to give in to destructive desires. Since this is an ongoing battle, there is a need for an ongoing support group to keep teaching the winning techniques to those who are in the midst of the battle. This material, as well as many other practical classes and support groups, should be constantly repeated so that healing and wholeness can be continually practiced.

Group levels:

As a pastor, I did find that I had three different levels of groups going through this kind of material in my church. The first group was the ongoing class that was a part of men's ministry. All men in the church were invited to attend this group. In this group all different kinds of men attended and were introduced to Biblical material to help in their battle with sexual temptation. The second level or type of group was a leadership development group. Each year I recruited men to be involved in small groups for intense spiritual and leadership development for a year. One of the sections of those groups was this material on Winning the Battle Over Temptation. The third level or type of group was a group that met weekly to be a support, recovery and training group for those who had addictive or habitual problems with sexual sin. Your church or organization may want to have different levels of handling this material also.

Spiritual Workouts:

At the end of each of the chapters of this book there are spiritual workouts. These Spiritual Workouts are designed to be a practical way of doing the truth of the Scriptures. Do at least one of the spiritual workouts at the conclusion of each chapter. Some spiritual workouts will be very powerful in your life while others will seemingly have no effect. But as is said at other places through out this book, it is the actual doing of Scripture that brings about life change. When you see the Spiritual Workout heading at the end of a chapter this is the signal that you are reading a way of actually doing the Scriptural truth. You may over the course of using the material invent a new way of applying the Scriptural truth that is not covered in the Spiritual Workout. Great! Write me and let me know, I would love to hear about it. If there is a better way of applying Scripture then we all win.

CLEANSE YOUR LIFE FROM PAST SEXUAL SINS

Step 1: Cleansing Sin Through Confession

The look of relief on his face was priceless. He had for the first time confessed to God that he had been involved in multiple affairs. After he had knelt down over the brown couch in his living room and poured out his heart to God, a whole new peace rushed into his life. God some how communicated to him that he was forgiven, because of what Christ had done. A new resolve entered his life that led him to deal with his life-long battle with pornography and adultery. He began to win when he began confessing how he had lost. One of the first things to do is cleanse your life of your sexual sins through confession to God based upon the life, death and resurrection of Jesus Christ.

In order to begin winning in your battle with lust, you must admit that you have sinned and are capable of it again. There is a tendency in all of us to deny the size and scope of our battle with sensual temptation. It is not that you simply slipped up in the past. You are in a struggle over what will control your heart, lust or love. You must admit that you are in a battle and that without help you will most likely give in and lose. This is not a battle that you can handle on your own. You need the Lord and you may need others.

In order to start winning against destructive desires you must make some admissions. **First**, you must admit where you have violated God's standards regarding sexual temptation and pleasure. **Second**, you must admit that you are capable of sinning and violating His standards in the future. **Third**, you must admit when you are under the pull of lust. These are called confessing in the Scripture. (1 John 1:5-10)

The first step for those who are serious about overcoming destructive desires is to cleanse their life from all their previous sexual sins. At the end of this chapter are various spiritual workouts that will allow you to comb through your life and confess your sins to God. God has defined where the boundaries of sexual conduct are to be placed. Sex is a gift that is too powerful to be held in anything other than its approved container, a life-time commitment between one man and one woman. When you have given into to sensuality and lust outside of marriage you are guilty before a Holy God. There are many ways to give in to lust that gives it a larger influence in our lives. We must take a long hard look at what God says about sexual sin, and where He wants us to draw the boundaries if we are to be free from lust's control. This is not an easy step to take, but it is essential if a person is to actually beat back the impact of lust.

You must admit that certain destructive desires are a temptress in your life and that at times it has won. Until you admit that lust has won some victories either mentally, physically or habitually, you will keep trying to rationalize why what you did is not that bad or that it is nothing compared to what another person is doing. Until you admit that lust has won at times or possibly quite regularly, you will never actually prepare for the next onslaught adequately. Until you fully admit when and where you have crossed God's boundaries for sexual conduct, you will not have His forgiveness and His power assisting you and guiding you. You must admit that you are in a real fight for control of what you think about, how you treat the opposite sex, and how far you will go to gain pleasure. Lust promises a short cut to intimacy and yet it can only deliver physical pleasure not true intimacy. At times you have given in to the bait and switch game of lust... substituting erotic stimulation for soul-satisfying intimacy.

You must understand what is happening to you when you give in to lust. It is the Ferrari body over the Volkswagen engine and undercarriage. It just doesn't perform in the way you wanted it to or needed. What you really long for and need is soul-stirring contact with someone who is completely open, accepting, encouraging and seeking your best. What lust offers is a temporary fix of a cotton candy high to a man in need of a real meat and potatoes meal. That is why it is possible for a person in the midst of a lust-generated sexual encounter to feel lonely.

You must also admit that you are being tempted either internally or externally by sensual thoughts or materials when this is happening. Denying that you feel the pull of this temptation is part of the problem. It must be exposed when you are under the influence of a tractor beam to strong inappropriate sexual expression.

Sensual and sexual sin is a spiritual, emotional and mental infection that becomes a malignancy spreading through your life if it is not dealt with effectively and thoroughly. There are three basic areas of sexual sin: **Sensuality and Lasciviousness:** sexual stimulation and sexual expressions outside of and/or before marriage; **Adultery:** sexual stimulation, sexual expression and sexual climax outside of the bounds of a public commitment of marriage; **Perversion:** sexual stimulation, sexual expression and sexual climax through twisted, distorted or aberrant interactions and involvements. In each of these areas the places where you have given in to lust needs to be exposed to the Lord for forgiveness, cleansing and repentance. As with any kind of infection it is not "fun" to expose the breadth and depth of the growing mass, but it is essential.

It is absolutely crucial that the power of cleansing, forgiveness and repentance become active in your life or your battle against lust has no chance of winning (Matt. 5:8; 1 John 1:9; 1 Thess. 4:1-8; Ps. 51). The forgiveness that resides in the death of Jesus Christ on the cross needs to be activated in your life through honest and sincere confession. While this seems like a daunting, even fearful, process, it is the first step toward healing and gaining power over lust in your life.

Understanding Sexual Sin

Sin is all forms of selfishness. The elevation of our wants, needs, desires ahead of God and others and at times at the expense of others. Destructive desire is just one form of selfishness that elevates SELF above all other things. God has provided for sexual pleasure, release and bonding through the life time public commitment of marriage. All forms of sexual sin are forms of sexual selfishness. In the most heinous forms of sexual selfishness the person wants the sexual pleasure that they want and will wound, use, abuse, molest or victimize others to get what they want. If your sensual impulse involves mainly what you want instead of how to minister to, how to benefit others, and how to glorify God, then your impulse is most likely selfishness.

A man is really facing three pressures to give into destructive desire. **First,** he is facing a physiological pressure: the build up of sperm every few days. **Second,** he is facing a contextual pressure: the sensual stimuli in our modern culture to build his life around sexual expression and conquest. **Third,** he is also facing the internal pressure of his own sin nature to just give into selfish pleasure.

We need at this point to discuss a basic physiology of sexual response and its impact on lust and temptation. When a young man reaches puberty he becomes physically programmed to be ready for sexual response every two to 5 days on average. (Every Man's Battle, Stephen Arterburn, p. 63, 64.) He has a production of about 100-200 million sperm every day. A man typically releases between 400-500 million sperm through the sexual release process (*http:kidzworld.com/site/p1863.htm*). Therefore we can conclude that God has designed a man to be drawn toward his wife a few times every week. This process does slow down with age. This natural build-up of sperm within the man predisposes him to a heightened alertness toward sensual material every few days. His body is geared toward releasing this sperm production in a sexual response to stimuli. If that man is not married or unable to enjoy physical intimacy with his wife, then he has a heightened internal orientation toward sexual material. His physical production of sperm does not mean he has to release or some harm will come to him. As one man said to me, "No one has ever blown up because he has an over production of sperm." It does mean that he will be more alert and susceptible to sexual temptation at the peak of his cycle. Because a man has a cycle does not mean that he has no choice but to give into sexual temptation if he is not married. This same logic would suggest that because a woman has a cycle and her emotions are tissue paper thin at points in that cycle she has to be mean, nasty and rude to people and there is nothing she can do about it.

While God's perfect design is for a man to release this build up of sperm through a caring sexual relationship with his wife, a man does not have to release this sperm production through sexual response. There are a number of other righteous ways of releasing this build-up of sperm. If a man is not married then he probably needs a high level of exercise, work and sleep to burn off all that sexual energy that he builds up regularly. God has also designed a man's body to release unused sperm in his sleep through night dreams or wet dreams. Furthermore, after a day or so without release the excess sperm will be reabsorbed into the body and the cycle will start again. Remember that a man does not have to give into lust and the mental framework of sensuality to fulfill a God-given need.

This build-up of sperm within the man means that he will be more susceptible to sexual temptation every few days. It does not mean that he has to give in, but he will face a greater temptation every few days. In other words, he becomes much more responsive to sensual pictures and images, sexual suggestion, mental fantasy, and external stimulation every few days. This is one of the reasons why it seems young men face a constant battle.

Some men realizing the relentless nature of their battle with destructive desires have completely given up. These three relentless enemies represent formidable foes. Do not despair. God has given us great weapons and great rewards if we will battle to become a loving person instead of just settling for a life of selfish lust. It is important to realize that the battle with destructive desires is one of the most focused places of the spiritual battle for a man's soul. It is here where he will beat back selfishness and live to God's glory and others' benefit. Or it is here that many men will surrender to selfishness and only put on a show of caring for anything or anyone but themselves. If you do not win this battle with lust, then your core will be selfish. And you will reap the consequences of a selfish life. We may lose a few battles with selfishness and with lust but God has sent His Son Jesus to die in our place for our sins and to empower us to be controlled by His love. We will receive everything we could ever want out of life if we learn to love God and others. Lust and selfishness seem like shortcuts to happiness and fulfillment, but they are not. They are actually shortcuts to a dead-end life of relational pain, separation, loneliness and lack of meaning. God has equipped us in Scripture and in the grace that is in Jesus Christ to win in the war against lust.

Women tend to face a slightly different battle with sexual temptation than men. Destructive desires for women often take the form of a perfect new man who will spend significant time focused on her. Just as men are tempted by a woman who appears to be ready to over-focus on his sexual needs, so a woman can be tempted by a man who will be all about a radicalized focus her relational needs. She longs to be highly valued and put on a pedestal, so he never ceases to praise her strong points. She wants a man to strive to understand her even more than she understands herself, so he is better than a psychologist at listening and having positive insights into who she is. She wants a man who will interact with her deeply and regularly about the topics that are interesting to her, so this new man is an incredible conversationalist. She longs for a man who will firmly but compassionately lead her, so this new man is a super talented leader focusing his leadership on her issues. She wants someone who will be a great dad for the children and deeply committed to the family, so this fantasy man is super-dad. She wants a man who will provide her with financial stability and even abundance, so this perfect man is rich and excited about her spending. This fantasy man is so perfect that a woman feels compelled to offer herself sexually to his talented love-making skills. The fantasy of this knight in shining armor who will do all these things creates a powerful temptation to live in a fantasy world and/or search for this man in reality. This fantasy man does not exist long-term in the real world. Just as the fantasy women of pornography do not exist in real life, so this fantasy man does not exist. If she allows herself to be pulled into this selfish world it will color her present world with cynicism and disrespect. Destructive desires try to lure men and women into a world where they are the center of attention. This world of selfishness is not love. It is not real and it cannot last long term.

chapter one

CLEANSE YOUR LIFE THROUGH CONFESSION

God describes each of the following as forms of sexual selfishness that He does not find acceptable: **Sensuality:** Gal. 5:19; **Lasciviousness:** Gal. 5:19; **Mental Adultery:** Matt 5:28; **Transvestitism:** Deut. 22:5; **Premarital Adultery:** Gal. 5:19; 1 Cor. 6:18; **Adultery:** Matt. 5:27-30; **Prostitution:** 1 Cor. 6:16-18; **Homosexual Episodes:** Lev. 18:22; 20:13; Rom. 1:26, 27; **Incest:** Lev. 18:6-18; 20:14; **Bestiality:** Lev.18:23; 20:15, 16; **Demonic Sexuality:** Gen. 6:4; Jude 1:6; **Sacrificial Sexuality:** Lev. 18:21; 20:6; Deut. 19:14.

Each of these sexual sins damages the individual, others, the society as a whole and God's glory. Each is a twisting or distortion of God's design for sexual relations and represents a level of selfishness that damages on a number of levels. God's plan and purpose for sexuality is that it be a form of caring for the other person and another way to psychologically, emotionally, spiritually and physically connect to your spouse. Unfortunately our society in its desire to allow selfishness to be given free reign has unleashed a whole new wave of sexual predators upon our society.

Our society has increasingly become lax in our understanding of what constitutes sexual sin. God's word however does not change and it is clear what God finds to be sexually damaging and sexually selfish. The beauty of sexuality within marriage is destroyed by selfish sexual desires. God is not being the great cosmic killjoy by placing sex outside of marriage on the morally repugnant list. He is placing these actions in the sinful list because they are selfish, because they victimize people, especially the innocent. He wants our best, and the fullness of what He has planned for our lives cannot be achieved if we move down the road of selfish sexual pleasure. You will destroy yourself and hurt a lot of other people also.

Many people, even Christians do not want to take an honest look at what God says is out of bounds in the sexual arena. Our society has become so permissive that we do not seem to be able to embrace the righteousness of God's standards in the sexual area. His laws, that were designed to protect us, our spouses, our children and the trust in communities, are seen as too restrictive and too old-fashioned. His boundaries which allow for deep satisfaction in marriage are viewed as impossible and even potentially harmful. Be prepared as you look at God's list of sexual selfishness to want to push back against it. In many parts of our society we have elevated sexual expression to a god. According to this thinking it is wrong, harmful, even intolerant to ask a person to hold back almost any sexual expression they feel the impulse to fulfill. This is nonsense and deeply destructive. Only when Christians begin to live righteous lives of loving purity will the world catch a glimpse of God's original plan for sexuality.

Look over the following list of sexual sins on the next few pages so that you can understand the scope of lust's temptation and destructive desires. If you have not heard of or been involved with a particular sexual sin mentioned in the list do not seek to understand the details of that sin, just realize that you have not committed that sin, (this is a good thing).

Destructive Desire	Scripture	Definition
Zone 1:		**Sensuality**
Sensuality:	Gal. 5:19	Contemplation, conversation, jokes or viewing of sexually explicit material.
Lasciviousness:	Gal. 5:19	Actions, words, behaviors designed to stir up inside of yourself or others—sexual ideas and actions which cannot be fulfilled within the context of marriage. This would include groping, indecent exposure, voyeurism, etc.
Mental Adultery:	Matt. 5:28	Mental images and stories and fantasies in which the individual participates in sexual practices with someone other than their spouse.
Transvestitism:	Deut. 22:5	This is where a person is trying to dress like a member of the opposite sex in order to stir up sexual desires within themselves or others.

Zone 2		Adultery
Fornication:	Gal. 5:19; 1 Cor. 6:18	This is when a person has sexual relations with another person before their public commitment of marriage.
Adultery:	Matt. 5:27-30	This is when a person goes outside the boundaries of their marriage to engage in sexual intimacy with another person other than their spouse.
Prostitution:	1 Cor. 6:16-18	This is when a person (usually a man) pays a person to have sexual relations outside of the commitment of marriage.
Zone 3:		Perversion /Distorted Sexuality:
Homosexual Episodes:	Lev. 18:22; 20:13; Rom. 1:26, 27	This is where a person pursues sexual expression and climax with a person of the same sex. This is a perversion of the nature of sexual expression and context as designed by God.
Incest:	Lev. 17:6-18	This is a perversion of sexual expression by having sexual expression and/or climax with one's family members or relatives.

Child Molestation:	Lev. 18:6-18; 20:14	This is a perversion of sexual expression by having sexual expression and/or climax with children under marriageable age.
Bestiality:	Lev. 18:23; 20:15,16	This is a selfish perversion of God's intended sexual expression by pursuing sexual expression or climax with and through animals.
Necrophilia:		This is a selfish perversion of God's intent for sexual expression by pursuing sexual expression and/or climax with the dead.
Incubus and/or Siccubus:	Gen. 6:4; Jude 1:6	This is a selfish perversion of God's intent for sexual expression by pursuing sexual expression, climax and/or procreation with spiritual beings.
Sacrificial Sexuality:	Lev. 18:21; 20:6; Deut. 19:14	This is a selfish perversion of God's intent for sexuality by pursuing sexual expression and climax through religious, occultic or satanic sexual rituals.

Spiritual Workout:
Confession of Sexual Sins

The process of breaking free from the promptings of lust starts with open and honest confession before God. While this is a difficult step it is essential to winning this conflict. A thorough job of confession includes agreeing with God that the sin is wrong and turning in a different direction both mentally and with your actions (1 John 1:9; 2 Cor. 4:1-4; Luke 17:3; Eph. 6:10-18)

Set aside about 30 minutes to an hour in a private place where you will be undisturbed to confess your specific sexual sins with the Lord Jesus Christ. Sit down with the list of sexual sins and perversions and make a mark or in some way indicate each time you have violated God's sexual boundaries. Do not write out a detailed story of each sexual sin. Just make a mark as an admission that you have committed that kind of sexual sin. It is usually helpful to throw away this marked confession sheet after your time of prayer. One may need to go over this list a few times in order to admit all the ways that you have been involved with sexual sin.

After the examination of your sexual sins it is important to agree with God in prayer that your actions were wrong and that you desire the forgiveness of Jesus Christ to cleanse you and energize you to live a life of purity. The following is a suggested prayer of confession. This is not a magical formula. It is your sincerity and honesty before God that is important. One does not have to use these exact words, but the ideas and motives are needed in a serious confession to the Lord.

Steps	Action Needed	Check When Completed
Step 1	Set aside 30 minutes to 2 hours for examination and confession.	
Step 2	Spend time being quiet before the Lord. Listening to worship music. Remind yourself that He is God.	
Step 3	Read over the list of sexual sins.	
Step 4	Put a dot or slash or code next to each area where you have been involved with sexual sin.	
Step 5	Spend some time grieving over your selfishness and violations of God's standards for sexual purity.	
Step 6	Pray a prayer of confession about your sexual sins. (See the suggested prayer that follows this table.) Be as specific as you can to the Lord without being graphic or sensational.	
Step 7	Receive the forgiveness that is Jesus Christ's death on the cross for you.	

Dear Heavenly Father,

I come in the name of the Lord Jesus Christ asking for Your forgiveness for my sexual sin. Lord Jesus, I agree with You that the sexual sin of   (list your specific sin)   is wrong. I turn away from it and ask that all the forgiveness that is in Your death on Calvary be applied to my sin in this area.   I give control of my sexuality to You, Lord Jesus. I ask You, Lord Jesus, to cleanse me of any and all unrighteousness (mental, emotional, physical and spiritual) that may cling to me because of my sin.

I ask You, Lord Jesus, that You would fill this area of my life with the Holy Spirit. Thank You, Lord Jesus, for dying on the cross for me. I fully acknowledge that only because of You do I have any forgiveness before God the Father.   I realize that only in Your power, energy and direction can I successfully turn away from this sin.

In the Name and for the Glory of the Lord Jesus Christ, Amen.

Spiritual Workout:
Confession of a Sensual Thought or Act

Confession of sin is not just a one-time event. Confession of sin is a daily or moment-by-moment process of making sure that we are right with God. If we give in to lust in our thought life, or through viewing pornography, or even actual sexual acts outside of marriage, we need to confess that sin to the Lord right away. It is best to keep short accounts with God. If you allow yourself to get away with giving in to lust over and over without going before the Lord in confession, then you will cut yourself off from deep fellowship with Him.

When a person is in close fellowship with the Lord there is an openness and intimacy between them. When God prompts you to do or say something, you say or do it. However when temptation, and specifically lust, enters the picture it tries to get you to pay attention to it rather than the prompting of the Lord and righteous living. If you give in to sin, then it is like a heavy fog begins to settle in on your relationship with the Lord and you cannot sense His presence or make out His direction for your actions. A number of years ago I had the privilege of leading a young woman to Jesus Christ as her Savior and Lord. She experienced becoming a Christian as an amazing transformation. She was delivered from a number of cravings, sins and addictions. A few months later she called me to say that she no longer felt close to the Lord and Christianity was not working. I met with her to explain that she had probably let sin win too many battles, and she was in the thick fog of disobedience and was sensing a distance between her and the Lord. She immediately said, "Yes, that is right!!!" "I fell back in to some old habits after seeing some friends." "I didn't realize that there was a direct connection between my enjoyment of the Christian life, intimacy with God, and my participation in sin." She confessed her sin on the spot and repented and moved directly back into a right fellowship/relationship with the Lord Jesus.

If you have given into sexual temptation, pray a prayer something like this:

Dear Heavenly Father,

I come to You, Heavenly Father, in the name of the Lord Jesus Christ. I want to admit to You that what I just did was not right. I gave in to lust and sexual temptation. I do not want to let lust dominate my life. I want to live a pure and righteous life of loving others. I confess that giving in to this temptation was wrong. I ask You to give me new power to resist the temptation the next time it might tempt me. I ask You to forgive me through the blood of Jesus Christ. I know that when lust was tempting me, You were prompting me (Gal. 5:16-19) to do something else, and I did not listen. I ask You to guide me to Your actions rather than lust . . . I will listen. Please strengthen me to see Your way of escape in the future. Thank You for being my Savior. I do want to please You.

In the Name of the Lord Jesus Christ,
Amen.

Spiritual Workout:
Confession of Perverse Sexual Sins

When dealing with sins in the perverse or aberrant category, there is often a level of emotional, psychological and/or demonic attachment and oppression that is associated with these sins. It is therefore necessary to make sure that the confession is thorough and the fleeing into the arms of Christ is complete. The following prayer is a more thorough and detailed prayer of confession and surrender to the Lord Jesus, in order to break any emotional, psychological or demonic attachments. You don't have to use these exact words, but these ideas of confession, repentance, renunciation, cleansing, and transfer should be present. This is not a magical formula; it is a suggested prayer. It is your sincerity and honesty before God that is important. In a few places there are fill in the blanks where you should fill in the sin you committed, and in some cases read the Scripture passage that declares a particular action displeasing to God.

Confession and Repentance: 1 John 1:9; 2 Tim. 2:24

Lord Jesus, I agree with You that _____ is wrong. I turn away from it and ask that all the forgiveness that is in Your death on Calvary be applied to my sin in this area. You say in Your Word that _____ is wrong. I realize that only in Your power and energy and through Your direction can I successfully turn away from this sin.

Renunciation: 2 Cor. 4:4

I repudiate, reject and renounce any ground, place or power I gave to Satan in my life through my involvement in _____ _____. I give to the Lord Jesus Christ all power over this area of my life. I willingly surrender this area to the Lord Jesus Christ and the Holy Spirit.

Cleansing and Expulsion: 1 John 1:9; Eph. 4:27

*I cancel out any contract I may have made with Satan through
_____. I ask you, Lord Jesus, to cleanse me of any
and all unrighteousness (mental, emotional, physical and spiritual) in answer to Your promise to cleanse me from all unrighteousness, if I would confess them to You.*

Transfer of Ownership and Infusion of the Spirit of Truth: 2 Cor. 10:3-5; Col. 3:1, 27, 28; Eph. 5:18

*I, right now, transfer ownership of sexuality and relationships
in my life to the Lord Jesus. I choose to take every thought
regarding sex, lust and sexual pleasure captive to Christ (2 Cor.
10:3-5) and allow Him full Lordship in this area. I ask You, Lord
Jesus, that You would fill this area of my life with the Holy Spirit
of Truth, so that I would be wise, thankful and able to see Your
plan in this area in the future. Thank You, Lord Jesus, for dying
on the cross for me. I choose to cooperate with You in the sexual area of my life, so that the process You began in me when
I first trusted in You can be completed (Phil. 1:6. I realize that
You want to display through me the character qualities of the
Lord Jesus (Col. 1:27, 28; Gal. 2:20).*

*In the Name and for the Glory of the Lord Jesus Christ,
Amen.*

In order for this prayer of confession to be maximally effective in breaking very strong sexual strongholds and influence, it is best if this prayer is prayed aloud with a mature Christian brother or prayer team present who is praying with and for you.

PREPARE TO RESIST TEMPTATION

Section 2: Prepare to Resist Sexual Temptations

There are essential preparations that need to be made so that when sexual temptation comes to lure you away from a Godly life, you are ready to resist and act righteously instead. If you do not prepare before the battle with temptation reaches its most intense times, you will lose and then have to reap the consequences. It is worth it to prepare. Remember if you are going to continue in right relationship with God and others, you must have a handle on lust in your life. You cannot be consumed by or with sexual pleasure. You must be able to recognize the signs of an enemy attack. Anticipating an attack and deciding ahead of time what you will do to resist is crucial to sustained victory. You must also be able to accurately perceive what God wants you to do and the needs of others. Remember that a righteous life of loving God and others first is the basis of a great life. The opposite of that which is a life lived to satisfy your own selfish pleasures, seems like a short cut to the good life but it is not. A me-first life will consistently sabotage your efforts to have a great life. ***LIFE IS RELATIONSHIPS*** and a life full of great relationships is built on loving God and others first. Then the rewards of a disciplined life just keep rolling in. Just as you would prepare in order to win a championship or winning presentation at work, so you must prepare to beat back the seduction of sexual selfishness. It wants you to waste your life chasing sexual arousal instead of accomplishing the great things God intends for your life to be about.

The writer of the book of Hebrews says, "**you have not yet resisted to the point of the shedding of blood in your striving against sin.**" He is challenging the Christians in Jerusalem to put more effort in to the ongoing battle with selfishness. If we raise the cost of giving in to sin we will avoid it. If we remind ourselves of the rewards of a life full of loving relationships we will avoid it. If we prepare for the various temptations that lust will approach us with, we will win in this battle.

1 Thess. 4:3

For this is the will of God, your sanctification; *that is*, that you abstain from sexual immorality; that each of you know how to possess his own vessel in sanctification and honor, not in lustful passion, like the Gentiles who do not know God.

chapter two

WINNING A WAR MEANS MANY BATTLES

Winning a war means many battles:

Jer. 12:5; Prov. 24:10; Matt. 26:40, 41; James 5:16

You will win some battles, you will lose some battles but you must keep fighting and push for victory in the war against lust. You are pushing for the ability to be pure and not consumed with selfishness towards others, especially the opposite sex. You are pushing to live a life of love rather than lust. Lust is selfish, a promised shortcut to intimacy of the deepest kind. Unfortunately it is a shortcut not to intimacy but to deeper selfishness and greater heartache. It is about what you want, and it hardens the person to aspects of love and caring. Every war is only won after many battles. Some battles will be lost even when you win the war. There is a need to celebrate each victory, even as we confess every defeat. Lust wants you to work for its impulses. It wants to capture you in an endless cycle of selfish pleasure, no matter how many others are wounded in the process. Just because we make a decision to live pure lives does not mean that purity will be ours immediately. We need to keep pushing toward purity. If there are setbacks, do not get discouraged, confess the problem, take responsibility for what you did, make whatever changes are necessary, and resist longer the next time and move more quickly to the loving counter action.

This is a war for your soul and there will be many battles, some which you will win and some which you will lose. Just as in World War II there were all kinds of battles, but the question was always how is the war effort going. The total view of the war was what was important. There were battles where the allied forces were routed. But this did not stop the generals, colonels and every fighting man from thinking about how they could win the next encounter. In the battle for your soul you will be lured into ambushes and traps. You will sometimes be deceived into walking into the enemy camp. You will have some battles with lust that you lose, but what matters is that you get up, confess the defeat, change whatever needs to be changed, and drive for the victory of real love in the future.

There was a young man who came to me after a significant defeat involving pornography. "I just couldn't seem to resist, so I gave in." He wanted to quit trying to be a Christian, leave the youth group and just live like a pagan. Being a Christian was too hard. It took a while to convince him to clean up the mess of the defeat (confession and repentance) and get back in the war ready to fight. We analyzed the defeat and made some changes in his routine so he was less vulnerable, and gave him some new spiritual weapons to resist temptation and pursue real love. He is winning the war, even though he has lost some battles.

I remember one man I was working with who had just lost in a battle with lust and had gone to visit a prostitute. He was so ashamed; he did not want to talk with me. He wanted to believe that he would never beat this problem with lust so he might as well just give in and stop trying to be a Christian. I remember talking with him for a couple of hours about his need to see the defeat in this battle as important, but not the outcome of the whole war. I was eventually successful at encouraging him to get back in the war and push for victory even though he had given in significantly.

Three passages of Scripture help us see the truth that we must be ready for many battles against temptation (Matt. 26:40,41; James 5:16; 1 John 1:8-10). Some of these battles will end in defeat in that particular battle. The ultimate victory is possible as we trust in God's power, direction and weaponry, but there will be times when temptation wins. It is not the end of the world, but a temporary setback. There will be more battles tomorrow, or next week, or next month.

We must prepare to win those battles, especially if we have just lost today's battle. Matt. 26:40, 41 says, **"And He came to the disciples and found them sleeping, and *said to Peter, 'So, you men could not keep watch with Me for one hour?' 'Keep watching and praying that you may not enter into temptation; the spirit is willing, but the flesh is weak.'"** Notice that Jesus is expecting the disciples to be in a battle in which they can win or lose. Notice that He also expects them to suffer some defeats with His **"the flesh is weak"** comment. Losing a few rounds to temptation is not unusual but expected. The key issue is whether you let a defeat destroy you or you see it as one small part of a larger war.

James 5:16 also tells us that we will at times lose battles to temptation and sin. **"Therefore, confess your sins to one another, and pray for one another so that you may be healed."** A part of winning the larger war is confessing our defeats to one another and encouraging one another to keep fighting. Prayer is directed to be used as a major weapon.

The Apostle John writing under the inspiration of the Holy Spirit also reinforces the idea that there will be many battles with some defeats in our Christian struggle. 1 John 1:8-10 **"If we say that we have no sin, we are deceiving ourselves and the truth is not in us. If we confess our sins, He is faithful and righteous to forgive us our sins and to cleanse us from all unrighteousness. If we say that we have not sinned, we make Him a liar and His word is not in us."** Everyone has the principle of selfishness and sin at work within them and everyone has and will sin from time to time. The fact that you suffered a defeat does not mean you should surrender, but rather you should strengthen yourself against that kind of attack in the future.

The church has not done a good enough job in many cases of helping real men with real sin and brokenness understand that there is forgiveness and redemption in the Christian community. We have often seen sexual sin as practically the unforgivable sin. Yes, giving in sexually to lust does limit one's ability to be used by God in certain roles. But until God calls a person home there is a legitimate role and place for them in the war for righteousness.

Spiritual Workout:

Pray a prayer of commitment to battling for a loving heart rather than giving in to selfish sexual pleasure.

Dear Lord Jesus, I realize that I will most likely be involved in a life long battle against sexual selfishness. I commit myself to winning this war and developing a loving lifestyle, one that looks to meet the needs of others and glorifies God. I will lose some battles but I ask You to empower me and teach me how to win the larger war through Your grace. I will not give up and surrender to selfishness just because I lost a battle or two. I will keep fighting no matter how intense the pressure. I will not become a prisoner of war to lust. I will not become an active agent of sexual selfishness. I want to honor You with my life. I want to live a life that allows Your love to control me.

In Jesus Christ name, Amen.

Pray a prayer looking for discernment and insight for future battles.

Dear Lord Jesus, I blew it and gave in to the temptation to lust. I don't want to lose these kinds of battles in the future, but I am not sure of all the reasons why I suffered this defeat. Please show me the reasons and insights I need to understand to win the next time I am faced with this temptation. Show me what I must do to protect myself against this type of temptation. In Jesus Christ name, Amen.

At this point you must be prepared to record the promptings and insights that the Lord will direct you to understand so you can actually pay attention to His guidance against this kind of temptation. Many times people pray a prayer of guidance and discernment but do not actually pay attention to the still small voice of the Holy Spirit answering the prayer.

chapter three

UNDERSTAND THE DIFFERENCE BETWEEN TEMPTATION AND SIN

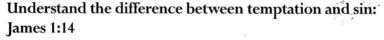

Understand the difference between temptation and sin: James 1:14

Christians must clearly understand when temptation becomes sin. The Apostle James says clearly that one is tempted when, **"one is carried away and enticed."** It is not wrong to be tempted. I know many Christians who are discouraged because they are being or have been tempted. Temptation is a part of living in a fallen world where selfishness is a viable option. Jesus was tempted the Scripture says, but He did not give into the temptation and sin (Heb. 4:15). Something inside of each of us wants to put ourselves first. If a temptation did not find any resonance within us it wouldn't be tempting. We will be tempted. We will want to give into the temptation. If we want to give in to sin, that does not mean that we have sinned, it means that we are being tempted to sin. It is crucial that you make that kind of distinction or you will believe you have sinned when all that has happened is temptation has found something that you want to do that is wrong. When we turn away from that which looks enticing to think and act and speak in a way that honors God and benefits others, we have successfully resisted temptation.

I have seen too many Christians who believe that because they want to give into the temptation, or because they have been tempted, they have committed a sin. All Christians face temptation, even sexual temptation. It is not wrong to be tempted or even to want to give in to that temptation.

Temptation becomes sin when you mentally, emotionally, or physically act on the sensual idea and go with its suggestions. Temptation is an impulse to do something that satisfies a personal pleasure at the expense of another. It is the suggestion to indulge in what God declares is wrong. Temptation does not become sin until it is embraced and acted upon, either mentally, emotionally or physically.

One man described temptation to his young disciple as ideas and actions flying around above his head. It becomes sin when you reach up and grab one of them. You cannot always control whether the temptations are flying above your head, but you can control whether you reach up and become active in thinking or doing the temptation.

Spiritual Workout:

FITNESS

In order to beat temptation you must be able to focus your mind on new thoughts rather than just be at the mercy of whatever thought comes into your mind. It is not sin to have the thought, but it becomes sin if you dwell on it or act on it. This will take mental discipline. Therefore you must practice thinking and acting in a different way than your dominant desire. Please fill in new thoughts that you will think about when you are tempted to dwell on lust, pornography, or sensual thoughts. I have included some possible new thoughts, but these are examples not necessarily what you will use.

Temptation:	Example:	New Thought:
Scantily Clad Woman	Family Member	
Mental Fantasy	Christ on the Cross	
Pornography	Work	
Computer Image	God Seeing You	
Previous Lustful Action	Future Goal	

It will take practice to force your mind not to give in to thinking about sensual material. This exercise usually points out how flabby and out of shape your mental muscles have become. Our minds often have become so undisciplined that we do not have control over what they think about. Our minds think about whatever they want to think about, and we have little ability to control what our minds focus on. To be a Godly person means that we have the ability to **"Set our minds on things above"** (Col. 3:1) and not on fleshly things. This takes mental practice in training your mind to focus on what is good and righteous.

chapter four

LOOK FOR THE LORD'S WAY OF ESCAPE

Look for the Lord's way of escape: 1 Cor. 10:13

God promises that with each temptation He allows to come our way He will provide a way of escape so that we will not have to give in to the dictates of selfishness. There is always a way out. You never have to sin. Most of the time we are being enticed into some selfish desire that pulls at us to surrender to our desires and wants instead of doing what is best for everyone, including ourselves.

Look at what 1 Cor. 10:13 actually says, **"No temptation has overtaken you but such as is common to man; and God is faithful, who will not allow you to be tempted beyond what you are able, but with the temptation will provide the way of escape also, so that you will be able to endure it."** This verse of Scripture tells us a lot about temptation. It tell us that temptation is a common experience for everyone. We all feel enticed to go outside of moral boundaries and be selfish. This verse tells us that when we feel the power of a temptation we are not the only ones who are enticed by this desire. Lots of people have felt this same desire. Even though we may be overwhelmed by our desire to give into a temptation, God does not allow us to experience a temptation that is so strong that it cannot be successfully resisted in some way. There is always a way of escaping the pull of the temptation so that it does not win. Remember there is always a God-provided way to keep the tractor beam of lust from winning, you have to be alert to it and take it when it is present.

It is important that we begin to look for and recognize God's way of escape. It could be that the way of escape is to turn off the computer and go to bed. It could be that the way of escape is to go out with friends. It could be that the way out of temptation is to decline the invitation to go out with certain friends. It could be that you need to do the dishes rather than just laze on the couch watching more television. It could be that you need to go to a small group meeting of people you know. It could be that you need to exercise. It could be that need to get up and walk. It could be that you need to phone a friend or mentor. It could be that you need to end the date before 11:00 pm. It could be any number of things that God will make you aware of... so that you can escape the power of that temptation. But many times we push away at the way of escape because we really want to have the temptation win. This is the difficult thing about temptation—it is pushing for us to give in to something we really want to do: the selfish part of ourselves: The I-want-what-I-want-right-now part of ourselves.

Spiritual Workout:

Think back on the last time you gave in to lust...

What were the ways of escape that God sent you but you ignored?

Think ahead and guess where lust will most likely begin tempting you.

What will the possible escapes be?

Where is temptation likely to come at you? (e.g. traveling, watching TV, Internet...)

What are the escape routes before you get there?

What are the escape routes from temptation at that place?

When is temptation most likely to come at you? (e.g. late at night, certain friends...)

What are the escape routes before you get tempted at that time?

What are the escape routes from temptation at that time?

Who are the most likely people you will be with when lust will be strong? (e.g. Girlfriend, opposite sex friend, friends, people connected to certain hobby...)

What are the escape routes before you are with this person?

What are the escape routes once your are with this person?

How is temptation most likely to tempt you in the next week? (e.g. TV, time with girlfriend/boyfriend, computer, magazines, jokes, email...)

What are the escape routes before this takes place?

What are the escape routes once the temptation has begun?

chapter five

PREPARE TO STAND FIRM IN THE EVIL DAY

Prepare to stand firm in the evil day: Eph. 6:13

There will be days when there will be lots of temptations and the battle is intense. It may be because the opportunity to give in to lust is stronger. It may be because something in your situation or activities triggers a lot of temptation. It may be that God has selected you to withstand a lot of temptation right at that time because of the global war. It may be that you are particularly vulnerable to the particular temptation that the Devil has ready in your life. But when the evil day comes it is essential that you depend upon the Lord and do everything to not give in. Temptation is trying to get you to deny your Christian commitment. Lust wants you to give in and begin living the selfish life. The Devil is very interested in you betraying the Lord and damaging your reputation.

Look at what Scripture says in Eph. 6:13, **"Therefore, take up the full armor of God, so that you will be able to resist in the evil day, and having done everything, to stand firm."** God tells us that we must have serious protection to withstand high level temptation that will come our way. Notice that there are periods or days when the work of the enemy is intense and constant. It is these intense and powerfully tempting days that we must make serious preparation for. There are days when resistance is victory. This is when progress is not possible but retreat is not an option. How does the old saying go? Momma said, "There would be days like this!!!" There will be times the Scriptures clearly declare when in your battle with lust it is all you can do to not give in. In these types of days and seasons it will not be possible to love more people or to make significant strides forward in godliness. It will be a victory to not give ground to the enemy.

I can remember working with a student who for two very intense weeks had two young ladies attracted to him who were being very aggressive about their interest in him. During this time, there was constant pressure and opportunity to give into sexual desires. Another different example is that most men experience a heightened interest in sex and sexual material when their bodies have produced an excess amount of sperm. During this one to two-day period, before release or reabsorption of the sperm, they are very temptable. One executive recounted to me that at one point a certain secretary was being very flirtatious and suggestive towards him at the office, and this represented the evil day for his battle against temptation. Realize that the devil is scheming to trip you up and have you move into selfishness rather than experience God's best for you. Therefore they have planned to bring the temptation that they think will be the most effective at precisely the time when you are the most vulnerable. Many businessmen have recounted to me that they face incredible sexual temptation and pressure when they travel, and this represents the evil day for them.

It is naïve to believe that there will not be days of intense spiritual battle over the control that lust has over you. You can be going along fine and then a huge ambush of temptation, lust and sensual opportunities trap you in a battle for your spiritual focus. Realize that the three enemies that you face in your battle with lust are capable of planning, strategizing and luring you into a trap, and then bombarding you with the most powerful forms of temptation specifically designed to make you give in. When that day comes, you must stand strong and refuse to give in. You must know what you will do when that day comes. You will need to add layers of spiritual armor to your life that you don't need during the normal periods of your life. During these intense times of attack and temptation you will need to alert people to pray for you and hold you accountable. You will not need to realize that you didn't do anything wrong which is causing you to be so tempted. It is just that God is allowing you to be tested so that you can move to the next level in your spiritual life. The world, the flesh, and the devil see it as an opportunity to sink the hooks of their control deep into your life.

Spiritual Workout:

FITNESS

List out 10 things that you will do when it is the evil day, and the spiritual battle for your soul in the area of lust is the most intense. (Hint: the techniques of this book are ways to stand firm.) This Spiritual Workout should be completed as you go through this book, but it should also be redone after you have tried out all the Biblical projects that are suggested in this book. You can then make a top ten list of Biblical projects that help you the most when you are facing intense temptation to give in to lust.

1.
2.
3.
4.
5.
6.
7.
8.
9.
10.

Practice using the above Biblical projects until you are skilled with them. These have proven to be effective, so become even more skilled with them so that you can do them as an instinctive reaction when lust attacks. Try them all out so that you know which ones work for you and which ones do not. You should not have to guess as to what you will do when the day of testing comes.

chapter six

PUT ON THE FULL ARMOR OF GOD

Put on the full armor of God: Eph. 6:14-18

If we were soldiers and were being deployed to an actual war zone, we would use every piece of armor and protection that was given to us. Unfortunately we do not realize that the Christian life is at times like a war. And at times we have been deployed into a real war zone where real causalities are possible. When you face those times and seasons of intense temptation from the devil, strap on the spiritual armor that God has provided.

Look at what the Scripture says to do when those days come. Eph. 6:11, 14-18 says, **"Put on the full armor of God, so that you will be able to stand firm against the schemes of the devil…"** **"Stand firm therefore, HAVING GIRDED YOUR LOINS WITH TRUTH, and HAVING PUT ON THE BREASTPLATE OF RIGHTEOUSNESS, and HAVING SHOD YOUR FEET WITH THE PREPARATION OF THE GOSPEL OF PEACE; in addition to all, TAKING UP THE SHIELD OF FAITH with which you will be able to extinguish all the flaming arrows of the evil *one*. And take THE HELMET OF SALVATION, and the SWORD OF THE SPIRIT, which is the word of God. With all prayer and**

petition pray at all times in the Spirit, and with this in view, be on the alert with all perseverance and petition for all the saints..."

Christians often make three mistakes when they look at this passage in Ephesians. Some focus almost completely on the historical pieces of Roman warfare and miss the actual truth God is teaching in this metaphor. Second, some Christian see this passage as symbolic of the struggle against general evil, instead of a fight against a specific foe with actual strategies and actual God-provided weapons and protection. Third, many Christians have not been taught to see this section of Scripture as a practical list of what to do when temptation is intense and persistent. This passage however is a dynamic listing of actual spiritual layers of protection. Do not focus on the Roman illustration of armor but on the actual spiritual protection that Paul details for us in this section. There are many things we can learn from an understanding of the Roman armor, but the focus should be on the spiritual armor.

The Apostle Paul is in a Roman prison as he writes these words, seeking to prepare and strengthen Christians in their real battle with the devil. He is trying to explain that God has given the Christian believer eight weapons in their fight with demonic temptation: standing firm, truth, righteousness, peace, faith, salvation, Scripture, prayer. He wants them to realize that these are not concepts or ideas or nice qualities, they are powerful usable weapons. Under the inspiration of God's Holy Spirit, he connects each of these weapons with a piece of armor that Roman soldiers wore. The illustration of Roman armor powerfully helps us see the battle. Unfortunately many Christians now spend too much time studying Roman military weaponry rather than the eight actual spiritual weapons God mentions in this passage. It is the spiritual weapons that will bring victory not the Roman equipment. We are facing a spiritual enemy, not a physical enemy like the Romans. God tells us to do at least eight things when we are spiritually attacked.

#	Reference and Verse	Explanation
1.	Eph. 6:14 Put on the full armor of God, so that you will be able to **stand firm** against the schemes of the devil... **Stand firm,** therefore.	**First,** stand firm, do not give an inch to the temptation, doubt, or attack that will rain down upon you.
2.	Eph. 6:14 Having girded you loins with **Truth,**	**Second,** remind yourself of the truth of the Christian worldview.
3.	Eph. 6:14 Having put on the Breastplate of **Righteousness,**	**Third,** reconnect to the righteous purity of Christ and eliminate any obvious unrighteous actions, thoughts and attitudes you are doing.
4.	Eph. 6:15 and having shod your feet with the preparation of the Gospel of **Peace;**	**Fourth,** re-embrace the peace with God that comes through Christ's death on the cross and make sure that you are not needlessly at odds with another person.
5.	Eph. 6:16 in addition to all, taking up the shield of **faith** with which you will be able to extinguish all the flaming arrows of the evil *one.*	**Fifth,** learn to trust God's sovereignty and love at a new level in spite of the attacks, temptations, doubts, hurts, etc., realizing that God will take care of what you cannot take care of.
6.	Eph. 6:17 And take the Helmet of **Salvation,**	**Sixth,** remind yourself of all of the benefits of salvation, the solutions that come from living a distinctively Christian life, and the wonders of a life in heaven with Christ.
7.	Eph. 6:17 and the sword of the Spirit, which is **the Word of God.**	**Seventh,** recite Scripture that deals with the temptations and attacks that we are facing.
8.	Eph. 6:18 With all **prayer** and petition pray at all times in the Spirit, and with this in view, be on the alert with all perseverance and petition for all the saints...	**Eighth,** pray and petition God for more direction, power, insight, discernment in order to win in this particular battle, and pray for other Christians that they would be strengthened.

Christians need to practice putting on the whole armor of God. Remember that in order for temptation to get into your soul, your spiritual armor must be down. These simple spiritual actions (Stand Firm, Truth, Righteousness, Peace, Salvation, Faith, Scripture, Prayer) are spiritual armor that make you able to resist temptation at a new level.

You will need to regularly practice these exercises so that you remain good at putting on spiritual protection and using spiritual weapons. You need to do this when temptation is not intense, so that when you are under great pressure your response will be more automatic. It is often too late to try to put this armor on for the first time when the temptation feels overwhelming. Let's take a little deeper look at these spiritual pieces of armor.

1. Stand firm: Practice taking no action, either mentally, or physically toward sin.

If a sensual picture is available for viewing, take no action to look at it. If a woman is flirting or being suggestive in some fashion, do not in any way signal with your eyes, face, mouth, hands or body that you are interested. Temptation is often trying to get us to compromise in seemingly unimportant little ways. But stand firm even on the small things. Do not purchase the cable package that includes sensual material. Do not try to get around the internet filter. Do not turn go to the sensual restaurant or entertainment when you travel.

2. Truth: Remind yourself again of the truth of the Christian Worldview. The Ultimate reality in the Universe is the Triune God. Above, beyond and before anything there is a Supreme Being we know of as God. He created the universe out of nothing, separate from Himself. He loved us enough to send His Son to pay the penalty for our selfishness and sin. He has communicated with us clearly and objectively without error in the Scriptures. He guides the Christian with His Holy Spirit. We can be forgiven of our sins and selfishness and have right relationship with God through belief in Jesus Christ's life and death. Jesus Christ died, was buried and rose from the dead. Mankind was created by God in His image, but now is corrupted with a natural inclination toward selfishness and sin. God has called each Christian to join with other Christians to worship Him, to grow in understanding and Christian living, to evangelize others, to deeply connect with others, to help the poor and afflicted. There is an after-life where heaven and/or hell will be the final real destination of individuals. History will have an end when Jesus Christ returns a second time and breaks into human history as ruler and King.

(See Appendix #3 for deeper treatment of this subject.)

3. Righteousness: Give thanks for the perfect life and death of Christ that allows God to establish a loving, accepting relationship with you. Eliminate anything you are doing that is clearly not righteous or pleasing to the Lord. Look for opportunities to meet the needs of others or benefit them in some way.

4. Peace: Re-embrace your acceptance of your absolute need of Christ's perfect life, death and resurrection. It is Christ's work that has allowed you to be at peace with God and nothing can separate you from His loving relationship with you. Remind yourself that your relationship with God does not depend on you but on what Christ has already done. Because of all that God through Christ has forgiven in you, stop fighting, hating, criticizing those who hurt, wound or slander you. Be at peace with others as far as it depends on you.

5. Faith: Commit again to trusting God's guidance, plans, lifestyle, and wisdom for your life. His way of life is a superior way of life for you. He is still in control. He can stop this difficult period whenever He wants. He loves you and will show you the way of escape. It is worthwhile to live God's way and trust Him.

6. Salvation: Force your mind to think again of what Christ has won for you through His life, death and resurrection. God chose you before the world began to receive His love and be in His family. You can relate to God directly because of the forgiveness of your sins. You are a member of God's forever family. God is work within you to make you more Christ-like. You have a home and citizenship in heaven. You are saved from facing the wrath of God. Christ is coming back for you. Heaven is where life will be revealed of which we only catch glimpses now. You have been given a guide for this life's path called the Holy Spirit. You find joy in purity instead of impurity. You have been forgiven. You will be given rewards for every Christ-like action you perform.

7. Scripture: Recite particular Scripture over and over again, under your breath, in your head or out-loud; verses like Ps. 119:9-11; 1 Thess. 4:3-5; 2 Tim. 2:22. Make little cards with these and other powerful Scriptures on them that you can carry with you all the time to refer to and read out loud when you face these times; or put them on your PDA so that you can refer to them quickly when they are needed.

8. Prayer: Ask God for strength to do the righteous thing instead of being sensual. Ask God to standing firm, truth, righteousness, peace, faith, salvation, Scripture and prayer. Keep praying for others until the power of the temptation is lessened and you can move on to other things.

Spiritual Workout

FITNESS

Put the lists and reminders and Scriptures of the previous exercises on a separate document so that you can refer to it in a moment's notice. Start putting on these pieces of armor by reading the lists, reminders and Scriptures out loud or under your breath. Do not be afraid to put on spiritual armor. It is not embarrassing to be tempted or attacked by lust. It is embarrassing to be bound hand and food by temptation and never put up much resistance. If temptation is attacking you, then you need protection.

Spiritual Armor	Spiritual Action
Stand Firm	Do not give in to sin at all in any way.
Truth	Remind yourself that there is a God who created the whole universe. Christ did rise from the dead. God did communicate with us in the Bible. Jesus Christ is coming back. He does forgive sinners because of Christ's death. The Holy Spirit does guide us. God does see everything we do. There will be a judgment day. There is a heaven to gain and a hell to lose.
Righteousness	Claim the righteousness that is in Christ. Do righteous, loving things. Get rid of whatever is not righteous in your life.
Peace	Make sure that you and God are at peace. Make sure that you and everyone else are, as peace at far as it depends upon you.
Salvation	Realize all God has done for you. Picture heaven and its wonders.
Faith	Declare that you are trusting God and His ways for sexual fulfillment and intimacy.
Scripture	Quote Scriptures you have memorized.
Prayer	Pray for others and ask God for strength to win the battle.

chapter seven

LOVE NOT LUST

Love Not Lust: 1 Tim. 1:5; Mark 12:30, 31

One of the key issues in battling lust is understanding what lust is trying to get you to not do. Lust is a form of selfishness. It does not want you to meet the needs of others. It does not want you to be an active agent for good in your world. Lust wants you to be self-absorbed, thinking about what you need and what you want. It wants you to focus on what will make you happy. To love is to meet needs, to please, to pursue. If temptation can get you to stop noticing another person's needs, then whatever you do will be selfish.

Your life opens up when you look to love instead of looking to receive. Look at what the Scripture tells us is the goal of life. 1 Tim. 1:5 **"But the goal of our instruction is love from a pure heart and a good conscience and a sincere faith."** Listen to what Jesus says about this same topic. The purpose or meaning of life is: **"...'YOU SHALL LOVE THE LORD YOUR GOD WITH ALL YOUR HEART, AND WITH ALL YOUR SOUL, AND WITH ALL YOUR MIND, AND WITH ALL YOUR STRENGTH.' "The second is this, 'YOU SHALL LOVE YOUR NEIGHBOR AS YOURSELF.' There is no other commandment greater than these" Mark 12:30-31.**

Now love is not a feeling, it is meeting the needs of others, pursuing the soul of another person, and pleasing another person. It doesn't matter whether I feel anything about meeting the needs of others, it just matters that I meet the needs. Our society has tired to change the definition of love from something I do for others to something I feel when others do things for me. We must go back to a Biblical definition of love. Lust wants us to give in to the selfish impulses in our lives. It wants us to build our whole life around the pursuit of our wants, desires and pleasures. If we fall for that lie, we will chase after selfish pleasure until it will no longer satisfy, and we become a perverted, lonely mess.

If instead of giving into lust's selfish desires, ask yourself and God, "Who has needs that I can meet?" You will live a richer and more rewarding life. At first lust seems to pay the greater rewards because you force the arrow of blessing to point your way. But eventually the only way that people will love you is if you pay them or force them. But if you meet the needs of others and pursue their souls, many of them will begin to willingly care for you and seek to bless you. You will be surrounded by mutual relationships of love.

Spiritual Workout:

FITNESS

Life moves forward when you love (Mark 12:29-31). Love is meeting needs. Therefore God wants you to be sensitive to the needs of others so that you can meet them, when it is appropriate. If we pay attention to the needs of others we will not be as susceptible to lust and selfish pleasure. There are 10 major relationships in your life. Look at each of these relationships and look for the needs that you can meet. If you will begin meeting the needs of others instead of seeking to have them meet your needs, you will begin enjoying real relationships and connection.

Relationships:	Questions:	Needs:
God	God has no needs that we can meet, but He accepts our praise, worship and service as love.	
Self:	What are your real needs at this point in your life?	
Spouse:	What does your spouse need from you in the marriage relationship?	
Family:	What are the basic needs of your family that you can meet?	
Work:	What are the needs of your company and the people in it that you can meet?	
Finances:	What are your basic financial needs?	
Church	What are the needs of your church and its people?	
Society and/or Community	What are the needs of your community that you can meet?	

Friends:	What are the needs of your friends that you can meet?	
Enemies:	Do your enemies have any needs that you can meet?	

Spiritual Workout

Pray and ask God what needs He is trying to make you sensitive to right now.

Spiritual Workout

Lust is a distraction. It is a diversion so that real love does not take place. If that is true and if you are feeling the pull of lust, there is a need that temptation is trying to keep you from noticing. What needs is lust trying to distract you from meeting? If lust can pull you away at the crucial moment to be selfish, then you will not be available to meet the crucial need in a loved one. What needs do those you love have that lust is trying to distract you from or make you unavailable for?

Lust is a Distraction

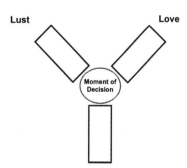

chapter eight

ASK FOR A NEW LEVEL OF THE HOLY SPIRIT FILLING

Ask for a new level of Holy Spirit control: Eph. 5:18; Gal. 5:16

I have sadly watched many men give over almost complete control of their lives to lust and sensuality. It begins with sexual desire suggesting "acceptable" thoughts and actions, but if these sexual urges are not resisted and controlled, the person eventually can become the slave of lust. Whenever and whatever lust urges them they obey. Some have disfigured their bodies, destroyed their marriages, infected themselves with diseases, discarded relationships, and/or destroyed their careers in order to obey the demands of lust within them. They become controlled by the impulses and desires of lustful activities. God has given us the antidote to this wicked control, the filling of the Holy Spirit. In many cases the only thing strong enough to overcome a person's pull to lust and sexual sin is a powerful infusion of the Spirit of the Living Christ. God commands that we ask for a new measure of the Holy Spirit, and then that we cooperate with that flow within us that prompts us to do righteousness. The filling of the Holy Spirit is not uncontrolled and manic like the filling of lust, but it is powerful. It will remake a person's life and overwhelm their old love of selfishness. The Christian is the person who is guided and controlled by the Holy Spirit. It is essential that we yield to God regularly and plead with God to fill us with His Holy Spirit at new levels. It is the depth of relationship with God that will allow us to overrule the allure of sensual relationships. A deep relationship with God delivers more than it promises. It is renewing, strengthening and draws blessing toward you. A lustful activity is a fraud. It delivers less than it promises. It drains, distracts and curses you into the dead end of increasing selfishness. The more filled that we are with the Holy Spirit, the more connected to God and other positive relationships we will be. Lust is trying to lure us toward shallow pleasure-centered relationships. God is offering to control us with His love (2 Cor. 5:14). One of the key ways of combating that is by having 3 dimensional relationships with God and with real people. When we are engaged in real give-and-take relationships with real people, self-centered, shallow interactions are not as enticing.

Look at what Scripture says in Eph. 5:18 **"And do not get drunk with wine, for that is dissipation, but be filled with the Spirit..."** This is a command. Be continually filled with the Spirit. Constantly ask and receive the wonder of God's abiding presence directing, strengthening, teaching and animating your life with a new level of Christ-like behavior. Pay attention to the power of the Holy Spirit residing within you. Do not grieve the Spirit by ignoring His advice, refusing His direction, or denying Him access to your hands, feet, mouth and mind (Eph. 4:30).

Yes, I know that many excesses and extremes have been allowed under the banner of the filling of the Holy Spirit, but I also know that God is not the God of disorder and excess. He is the God of decency, order and power. He came to set the captive free. We do not have to fear giving over control of our lives to God. He loves us and has a wonderful plan for our lives. As we walk with Him and cry out for a new measure of His Spirit just like Elisha (2 Kings 2:9), He will answer and empower us for the purpose He has called us. Lust seeks to possess us and have us do its bidding. God loves us and seeks to empower us to do His will so that He can reward us. In Eph. 5:18 the phrase "be filled with the Spirit" is a present tense command which means that we are to constantly be filled with the Holy Spirit. We are not strong enough to live the Christian life on our own. Receiving a new level of filling of the Holy Spirit is not a bombastic thing—it is an energizing thing. Do you think the car feels more powerful when a new engine is put under the hood—no it just performs better.

Many men have surrendered to the spirit of lust. When it prompts them to fantasize, they fantasize. When it prompts them to look at pornography, they look at pornography. When it prompts them masturbate, they masturbate. When it prompts them to take the next step down the road of sexual desire, they take that next step. The question that needs to be asked is when was the last time that you successfully resisted the spirit of lust by saying no to its impulses to sexual desire. The Spirit of the Living God and the spirit of lust are battling for control of your soul, and you are slaves of the one whom you obey (Rom. 6:16, 17). God calls us to continually give over control of our lives the Holy Spirit and obey His righteous promptings and direction. It grieves the Holy Spirit when we obey the spirit of our flesh in any form: anger, pride, lust, sorcery, envy, etc. (Eph. 4:30).

Spiritual Workout:

FITNESS

Ask the Spirit of the Living Christ to take over more of your life every day. Yield yourself to a deeper relationship with the Holy Spirit every day. Just as you would change your schedule, your conversation and your lifestyle if someone really special or important started to spend time with you, in the same way ask the Holy Spirit to fill every aspect of your life and adjust to your life to Him. Ask Him to comment on every activity, every relationship, every conversation. Ask Him what would please Him and what displeases Him. There may be some relationships, activities and ways of communicating that need to go. There may also be something that needs to be added.

Dear Lord Jesus Christ,

I ask you to fill me with a new measure of Your Holy Spirit, today. I want to be controlled by Your love and Your direction. I yield myself to the prompting and wisdom of the Spirit of the Living Christ who died on Calvary. I give You permission to make me the kind of person You want me to be.

In Jesus Christ name,

Amen.

chapter nine

FIGHT TEMPTATION ON THE RIGHT BATTLEFIELD

Fight Temptation on the Right Battlefield: 2 Cor. 10:5

I have worked with dozens of men who have been caught in all kinds of sexual sins: sensuality, prostitution, pornography, fornication, adultery, homosexuality, molestation, rape, seduction, etc. With each one of them I have taken them back to the battle in their mind. It is here that all successful struggles with lust must begin. The battle is for what you think about. If you do not begin battling in your mind then you cannot win. Lust wants to become an addiction in your life. It wants to have you act out your sexual fantasies. Lust wants to have you give in to its impulses in major ways. You will not win in your battle with lust (no matter how much you have given in to temptation) by resisting the major sexual actions or by cutting back on pornographic use. The way you win is by entering into the battlefield of your mind and winning there. You will never win in your battle against lust and sexual selfishness until you begin turning away from it in your mind. You will win or lose the battle in your mind well before you face the battle in your actions or habits. So you must go back and begin fighting the battle on that battlefield. You must do everything you can to begin winning against lusts mental temptations.

2 Cor. 10:3-5 declares the key battleground in this war against temptation: the mind. **"For though we walk in the flesh, we do not war according to the flesh, for the weapons of our warfare**

are not of the flesh, but divinely powerful for the destruction of fortresses. _We are_ destroying speculations and every lofty thing raised up against the knowledge of God, and _we are_ taking every thought captive to the obedience of Christ." It is imperative that we keep the battle with lust contained to the mind. If we allow ourselves to begin fighting on multiple battlefields then we incrementally lose more ground.

If you are fighting the battle against lust in your thoughts and you give in or surrender, then you will begin battling in your actions. You will begin doing some sensual, lustful or sexually selfish action that you were not doing before. If you begin battling this action and other sexually lustful actions and lose that battle, then you will begin to have a habit/pattern of lustful surrender. That surrender allows lust to have an addictive beachhead in your life to expand the influence and control of lust in your life. If you have an addiction to pornography or prostitutes or adultery or some other sexual sin, then you will not win by just cutting back. You must go back to the source of the problem, what you let your mind think about. You must begin to force your mind to think about pure and righteous, loving actions towards others. You must make sure that your mind does not give in to long periods of sexual fantasy. If you are unwilling to begin fighting the battle against lust in your mind, you cannot win.

Spiritual Workout:
Three Battlefields

Which battlefields are you fighting on?

_____ Mind _____ Actions _____ Habits

What are three weapons that lust uses to get you thinking about sensuality?

What are you going to think about other than those thoughts?

How are you going to keep your mind from giving in to lustful fantasies?

Dear Lord Jesus,

I, _____ am prepared to do battle in my mind against lust and not just try to stop doing lustful things. I ask for Your grace as I bring You each thought and seek to build a whole new way of thinking. I wait for Your direction, energy and guidance. I will not longer surrender the high ground of my mind in this battle against lust.

In the Name of the Lord Jesus Christ,

Amen.

chapter ten

HONEST ASSESSMENT OF YOUR INVOLVEMENT IN PORNOGRAPHY

Honest assessment of your current involvement in Pornography: Gal. 6:7; Prov. 23:27

Many men struggle with significant temptation and lust because they have stopped seeing their involvement in pornography as wrong and contaminating. Scripture says that giving into lust and adultery is like diving head first into a narrow well (Prov. 23:27). After a while, swimming in a filthy pool ceases to become shocking. How low are you already diving in the cesspool of pornography? Not only is lust and adultery a narrow well, it is also a narrow well full of filth. It is a cesspool. It is full of disease, loneliness, broken relationships, lies, mistrust, and destroyed reputation. You won't be able to turn around and you will most likely drown in there. Listen to God speak in Gal. 6:7, **"Do not be deceived, God is not mocked; for whatever a man sows, this he will also reap."** Many people do not understand that their actions are seeds they sowing that will grow into their life. If you sow selfishness as your dominant crop, your life will be filled with bitterness and damaged relationships.

Richard Dobbins from Emerge ministries has suggested that there are 5 levels of involvement in pornography. We must take a hard look at how deeply we may have been drawn into interaction with pornography in its various forms. I have taken Dr. Dobbins and given my definitions to his levels of involvement. I encourage you to check out Dr. Dobbins ministry and materials.

Level 1: Curiosity: this is where a person allows their curiosity to pull them into viewing a type or form of pornography. There is not a repeated use. Usually one is shocked and shamed by what was seen.

Level 2: Experimentation: this is where curiosity has yielded to occasional involvement. It is not regular or consistent. It is no longer curiosity, because you know what you will find if you go to that web site or that store or open that e-mail. You are experimenting with its impact on you.

Level 3: Regular Use: this is where you view pornography on a regular basis. It could be every weekend. It could be every time you are on a business trip. It could be each time a certain kind of e-mail comes. It could be on a regular basis as a tool for sexual release. It is at this level that you begin to need help to pull back. If you are at this level you seriously need to think through bringing a trusted confidant into your amount of usage of pornography so you can stop.

Level 4: Habitual Use: this is where you view pornography almost every day. It is just a part of your life. You almost always will look at a porn site when you are on the computer. You will view pornography at work even though you are not supposed to. You have magazines, videos, etc at easy reach. This is a serious level of involvement and colors your view of marriage, women, yourself and your world. It will almost always require that you have at least one if not more men helping you become free of this level of involvement in pornography. A clear mind is possible. You do not have to be controlled by the impulses to view or act out sexually explicit scenes.

Level 5: Addictive Use: this is where a person uses pornography to make themselves feel better. It is a medication to cover over a wound, a trauma, a painful memory. When there is something extremely painful in our lives that we don't want to face we try to cover it over with alcohol, drugs, food and even pornography. Whatever will cause us to forget the pain. This requires a support group and a trust in God to conquer lust at this level. He can set you free and He can help you face whatever you are running from.

Realize that pornography keeps seducing people into more and deeper levels of use. If you do not take serious and practical steps to stop your increasing involvement it will become a huge problem in your life. "Do not be deceived, God is not mocked whatsoever a man sows that shall he also reap." If you are at level 1 or 2 you may be able to get out by yourself, but if you are at level 3 and beyond, you need some help to get out of this pit of sin. Pornography and lust are trying to deceive you into believing that giving in to viewing sexually explicit stories, images, movies, and/or games is normal and natural. If you are not careful you will be lured into a major problem through little surrenders until you are at the bottom of a narrow well with few ways out, and serious damage to your soul and your relationships.

Spiritual Workout

Where are you on the 5 Levels of involvement in Pornography?

_____ Curiosity:

_____ Experimentation:

_____ Regular Use:

_____ Habitual Use:

_____ Addictive Use:

If you are past the first two levels of involvement in pornography (Curiosity or Experimentation) please let at least one person know about your involvement with pornography. It should be a person you respect and who can keep your information confidential. It is best if it is a person who can keep you accountable for doing these exercises.

Ask this person to pray with you. _____

Who are you going to talk to? _____

By what date will you tell them? _____

Ask this person to work the projects of Breaking Free From Lust with you.

Spiritual Workout

If you are past level two you need more specific and often ongoing help to swim out of this cesspool. Write down the what, who, where, when, how of these essentials to a winning battle plan against lust.

Books, Articles, Information:

Scripture Verses memorized and meditated upon:

Counselors:

Small Group:

Mentor/Sponsor:

Weekly accountability to do the Breaking Free From Lust program in this book:

Computer Filter and Accountability:

chapter eleven

BUILD A CATALOGUE OF POSITIVE MENTAL "MOVIES"

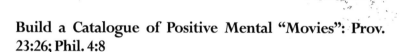

Build a Catalogue of Positive Mental "Movies": Prov. 23:26; Phil. 4:8

Many men do not have a group of positive mental movies to go to when they are tempted, so they just go with the fantasy that has popped up in their mind. In order to defeat the mental images of lust and sensuality that temptation wants a person to dwell on, it is important to have a list of great achievements, good moments, pure images, and positive times that you can force your mind to focus on, rather than having the powerful images of lust take over your thinking. These mental pictures need to be thought through ahead of time so that you are not left fumbling mentally when temptation comes and wants you to think its way. The Scripture says, **"Finally, brethren, whatever is true, whatever is honorable, whatever is right, whatever is pure, whatever is lovely, whatever is of good repute, if there is any excellence and if anything worthy of praise, dwell on these things."**

Write out ahead of time the various mental "movies" that you will play in your head so that your mind will be controlled by righteousness rather than sexual selfishness.

Prov. 23:26 says, **"Give me your heart, my son, and let your eyes delight in my ways."** The word for heart is the Hebrew word *leb* which means the inner part of man, the invisible part of a person, the soul. If we are to defeat the pull of lust then we must have our minds full of that which brings delight to the heart of God. It is our renewed mind that will allow us to pursue purity and not be sucked aside into lust and selfishness.

Spiritual Workout:
Building a Catalogue of
Positive Mental Movies

Make a list of positive moments in your life that you can relive whenever temptation presses on you to give into lust and sexual selfishness. These could be times of great personal triumph or just good times. These could be times when you were close to God or some other positive experience. Write down the positive events in your life:

Age	Positive Memory
0 – 10	
11 - 20	
21 – 30	
31 – 40	
41 – 50	
51 – 60	
61 – 70	
71 – 80	
81 – 90	

FITNESS

Spiritual Workout:
Building a Catalogue of Positive Mental Movies

In each of the following categories, write down at least two scenes or mental images that you could focus on instead of giving in to sexual fantasy and lustful images. Go through the mental, emotional and physical discipline of doing this exercise and you will be more prepared for your next time of temptation.

Questions	Answers
What are two emotionally satisfying scenes with your Family?	
What are two emotionally satisfying scenes with Sports?	
What are two emotionally satisfying scenes with your Work?	
What are two emotionally satisfying scenes with your Hobbies?	
What are two emotionally satisfying scenes in the Bible?	
What are two emotionally satisfying times with Spouse?	
What are two emotionally satisfying scenes with your Family?	
What are two emotionally satisfying scenes with Travel?	
What are two emotionally satisfying scenes about your Dreams/Goals?	
What are two emotionally satisfying scenes with your Favorite places?	
What are two emotionally satisfying scenes with Cherished Memories?	

What are two emotionally satisfying songs in Music?	
What are two emotionally satisfying scenes with Scenes from Movies?	
What are two emotionally satisfying scenes in Books?	

Some people carry a list of the top 10 of these positive mental images on a little card so they can refer to it when they need to. When they are pressed by temptation they pull out the list or pictures of those events and it keeps them from giving in to lust.

#	Top Ten Righteous Emotionally Satisfying Scenes
1.	
2.	
3.	
4.	
5.	
6.	
7.	
8.	
9.	
10.	

chapter twelve

REMOVE HIDDEN PROVISIONS FOR DEFEAT

Remove Hidden Provisions for Defeat: Rom. 13:14

I remember one man I was working with who had a huge collection of sexually explicit magazines that he had collected over the years. I told him that if he was going to really make progress in his battle with lust he was going to have to get this stuff out of his house. He did and yet he was not making much progress. It took me about a month to realize that he removed the magazines from his house but had put them in his truck. He did not want to get rid of them because they were worth a lot of money. He was making a hidden provision for defeat by the flesh. Get serious!

Many people say they want to win against lust, but they leave tempting materials, access, activities in their lives knowing that these will come up and lead them to a fall. If you are really serious about moving past lust to love, then you must be ruthless in your elimination of hidden aids to temptation. Just like an alcoholic may hide a fifth of vodka in the toilet tank for hidden use later, so those wanting to pretend they want no part of lust hide explicit magazines or refuse to put blocks on their web surfing. If you are serious then get rid of all the secret places where you know you have hidden lustful temptations. Get rid of the usual places where you access this material.

Scripture says, **"But put on the Lord Jesus Christ, and make no provision for the flesh in regard to *its* lusts"** (Rom. 13:14). In order to really begin a battle with lust we must eliminate the secret things we hide that allow us to give in to temptation. We must remove and/or destroy the books, movies, cable channels, magazines, pictures, stories, even mental images and any other sensual material that we may occasionally use to give in to sensual temptation and lust. It is not uncommon when a person gets serious about battling lust that they pull out of various places a whole host of things that need to be destroyed. I have watched this process a number of times and it always marks a significant break from the pretence of the past.

One man told me that he did not really begin to make progress in his sexual addiction to pornography until he installed a slower modem on his home computer and told his wife that he was most tempted to look at pornography after 10 p.m. at night. So they set up the rule that he could not be on the internet after 10 p.m. and they kept the modem speed really slow on the home computer.

Another young man I was working with was the most tempted to engage in lustful behavior by television programs that came on after his roommates went to sleep. He worked swing shift so he would get in after midnight and watch something to unwind. This inevitably moved to other more provocative programs. We were able to enlist the help of his roommates, and they removed the knobs from the television and the cord so that it could not be turned on after they went to sleep.

Most often, surrendering to a temptation means that we have made it too easy to surrender. If we leave tempting materials or easy access to that material in our homes, at work or other areas we regularly go to, then we are playing a game that we will lose. Only when we do what God asks, "Make no provisions for the flesh to fulfill the lusts thereof…" (Rom. 13:14). Think through the typical ways that you begin being tempted or giving into lust. Does it start with a certain friend? Does it start at a certain time? Does it start with a particular activity?

Spiritual Workout

FITNESS

Think through the typical ways that you begin being tempted or giving in to lust. Does it start with a certain friend? Does it start at a certain time? Does it start with a particular activity? What do you need to get rid of that no one or only a few people know about? Go through your house and clean out anything that could be a prompt to lust and inappropriate sexual desire.

- Magazines
- Books
- Unfiltered and Unaccountable Computer Access
- Cable TV Channel
- Friendships
- Recreation
- Particular Activity

Get rid of those things right now!!!!

chapter thirteen

PERSONALIZE ROMANS 6:1-23

Personalize Rom. 6:1-23

One of the most powerful meditations that anyone can do to strengthen themselves against the power of temptation is to personalize Rom. 6:1-23. There is power in the Word of God and ruminating on it through writing it out. Write out the verse thought-for-thought, putting your particular temptation in every place where it mentions sin. I have been suggesting this way of strengthening yourself against the temptation for years. Almost everyone who does this spiritual exercise is amazed at how much power there is in this form of meditation. When a person will write out the whole of Rom. 6:1-23 every day until the season of temptation is over, this will go a long way to empowering a purity. When temptation is particularly strong I have recommended that you write out Romans 6:1-23 at least once a day, if not a number of times each day. Some have found that three to five times per day can be very helpful in intensive situations (waking up, breakfast, lunch, dinner, before sleeping).

Spiritual Workout:
Personalize Rom. 6:1-23

Write out Rom. 6:1-23 inserting lust in each place where sin is mentioned or possible. Insert your own name in every place where you can place it. Keep writing out this chapter of Scripture every day until you are strengthened and lust does not come at you so strongly each day.

Memorize Romans 6:1-3 and repeat it throughout the day, putting lust in the place of the word sin. If you can quote this verse and regularly repeat it, it will strengthen you.

Memorize Romans 6:11-13 and repeat it throughout the day, putting lust in the place of the word sin. If you can quote this verse and regularly repeat it, it will strengthen you.

What do you say then Bill? Are you going to continue lusting so that grace may increase? How stupid Bill! How shall you, Bill, who died to lust still live in it? Or do you not know that everyone including you Bill, who has been baptized into Christ Jesus have been baptized into His death? . . . Consider yourself dead to lusting Bill. Stop letting lust tell you what to do, Bill. And stop giving lust the parts of your body to use: your mind, your hands, your mouth, your eyes . . . Bill, lust doesn't have to be the master over you with you obeying its every suggestion. Listen Bill, if you do what lust wants all the time, then you are the slave of lust. The more you obey its promptings, the more bondage and slavery you will be in. Stop doing what lust wants, do what Christ wants.

chapter fourteen

CONFESS YOUR SINS WHEN YOU COMMIT THEM

Confess your sins when you commit them: 1 John 1:9

One of the important things to remember in our discussion of the battle against lust, you will not win every battle. You will sin, but God has given each one of us an incredible gift. It is the gift of access to the forgiveness of God. Access to the forgiveness of God is CONFESSION OF SINS. The forgiveness of God is made available by the death of Christ on the cross as our sin substitute, but it is activated in our life by our admission of our need and our agreement that He was right and we were wrong.

I have watched many young people get all excited about battling against sensual temptations. They mistakenly embrace the idea that because they are sincere, energetic and praying, they will never suffer another defeat. This is not realistic. Unfortunately you may give in to temptation in some form. Hopefully it is only a small surrender. But whether it is small or big, you must realize that this is a war not an individual battle. If you made mistakes, correct them. If you sinned, confess. If you were deceived, repent of your naiveté. Realize that it is important that you begin loving others again rather than sinking into a selfish pit where it is all about you. Some people have been devastated when lust wins a battle. Do not be destroyed. Confess the sin, repent of the mindset and get back in the business of loving God and loving others. God has anticipated that you will not win every battle, so He gave us confession to access forgiveness.

Spiritual Workout:
Confession of a Sensual Thought or Act.

Confession of sin is not just a one time event. Confession of sin is a daily or moment-by-moment process of making sure that we are right with God. If we give in to lust in our thought life or through viewing pornography, or even actual sexual acts outside of marriage, we need to confess that sin to the Lord right away. It is best to keep short accounts with God. If you allow yourself to get away with giving in to lust over and over without going before the Lord in confession, then you will cut yourself off from deep fellowship with Him.

If you have given into sexual temptation, pray a prayer something like this:

Dear Heavenly Father,

I come to You in the name of the Lord Jesus Christ. I want to admit to You that what I just did was not right. I gave into lust and sexual temptation. I do not want to let lust dominate my life. I want to live a pure and righteous life of loving others. I confess that giving in to this temptation was wrong. I ask You to give me new power to resist the temptation the next time it might tempt me. I ask You to forgive me through the blood of Jesus Christ. I know that when lust was tempting me, You were prompting me (Gal. 5:16-19) to do something else and I did not listen. I ask you to guide me to Your actions rather than lust . . . I will listen. Please strengthen me to see Your way of escape in the future. Thank You for being my Savior. I do want to please You.

In the name of the Lord Jesus Christ,
Amen.

chapter fifteen

COVER UP THE SENSUAL IMAGES IN YOUR MIND

Cover up the sinful images in your mind: 2 Cor. 10:3-5

It only takes a few seconds for a man to memorize a picture of pornography or record a permanent image of a sexual act in his mind. These images act like an internal porn gallery that stirs up a man to be selfish. It does not seem possible to remove these images from our mind since they have strong emotional and sexual connections. The more we focus on not thinking about them, the stronger they become. What is needed is to cover over these images with stronger, more emotional, psychological and spiritual images. We can force our minds to put over those sensual pictures, images that will bring us back to true Spiritual reality. The images that we use to cover the sensual images should include the destructive consequences of doing the sin we are picturing.

We need to look again at this pivotal passage in 2 Cor. 10:3-5, and draw out another application for our practical use. **"For though we walk in the flesh, we do not war according to the flesh, for the weapons of our warfare are not of the flesh, but divinely powerful for the destruction of fortresses. *We are* destroying speculations**

and every lofty thing raised up against the knowledge of God, and _we are_ **taking every thought captive to the obedience of Christ."** The sensually provocative images that we have stored in our minds are fortresses of sin. They represent speculation and something raised up in our soul that is against the complete rule of Christ. So these images must be closed and no longer used. Their allure and power must be shut down. Covering over these images with powerful images of the results of sensual sin shuts down their seductive power. Forcing ourselves to see the spiritual consequences of going down the sensual road stuns us and makes us turn back. We cannot allow ourselves to contemplate sin in a consequences-free environment as though doing sin has no consequences, only benefits. We need to challenge the sensual ideas, pictures and scenarios with reality, deep spiritual truth, and the shocking results that occur two years after the pleasure.

Many people feel as though what they think about is private and it does not matter whether we contemplate sin as long as we don't act on it. This is faulty thinking. Your soul is the place where you actually live and each sensual image is a toxic substance oozing its poison into your thinking, will and emotions. What you think about affects how you live and how you approach the world. If you allow the toxic impact of personal sexual gratification to exist freely in your mind, then elements of this selfish contaminant will leak into your speech, your actions and your attitudes. You will lose focus on the righteous action if you allow your mind to create powerful scenarios of lust. Sexual fantasy, except with your spouse, pollutes the mind and primes the body for the wrong actions.

Build Powerful Pictures of the Results of Lust

Some of the most powerful pictures for covering over sensual images are Biblical images or images of the long-term results of sexual sin. One could picture David having no power with God, his family, or the nation because of his adultery with Bathsheba and murder of Uriah. The picture should include his weeping and seeking God's face as he watches his family fall apart. You could picture Sampson who was so unable to curb his lust that he slept with whatever prostitute would have him. His ministry was destroyed. He was captured by the enemy and had his eyes gouged out. You could picture the Lord Jesus Christ on the Cross and you as one of the soldiers that is nailing Him to the Cross. You are crucifying Him because you insist that you be allowed to indulge your selfish, sexual fantasy. You could picture yourself as an Old Testament worshipper putting your hands on an innocent lamb and announcing your sin – SENSUALITY OR LASCIVIOUSNESS, OR MENTAL ADULTERY, OR FORNICATION, OR ADULTERY—and then feeling the priest reach around the neck of the animal and slit its throat as the payment for your sin. You feel the life of the animal drain away. As you peel the head back of the animal that paid with its life for your sin, you see the face of Christ.

Spiritual Workout:

FITNESS

Picture yourself nailing Christ to the cross: Someone has to pay for your lust and sexual selfishness—it was Christ. Hold down His wrists and drive the nails through them. Hear Him say, "I forgive you. Now go and sin no more." Picture Him hanging on the cross suffocating to death because of your giving in to lust.

Picture the destruction of your sons and your daughters: Your children are more prone to giving in to the sins that you do not learn to conquer. Create the mental picture of the future and how lust will mess up their lives. Just like David destroyed so much of his family through his lust. He set off a chain reaction of murder, intrigue, rape, destruction, betrayal. So your lust does the same thing in your family. You need to picture the potential devastation that could result from your giving in to lust.

Picture yourself holding the head of a lamb and confessing your sexual sins: Then the priest slits the throat of the animal and you feel its life drain away because it has been your substitute. Picture yourself peeling back the head of the animal to reveal the face of Christ. He is your lamb from God who takes away your sin. Do you want to go on crucifying Him with your sins?

Picture Sampson who became the slave of lust: If a woman looked good to him he allowed her to redirect him from doing the will of God and fulfilling the purpose of his life. See the Philistines holding him after Delilah had his hair cut, and gouging out his eyes, because they knew that it was his eyes that made him give in to lust. Picture this champion of Israel reduced to grinding wheat like an ox, instead of winning great victories for God. Picture the defeated and blind Sampson depressed in the dungeon grinding wheat because he could not control the impulses to lust.

Picture Demas running away from Christ, Paul and eternal rewards: Demas had the privilege of traveling with the Apostle Paul and seeing miracles and watching God's power displayed. Picture him as he gave up the privilege of spiritual power and the presence of God for the passing fancies of a beautiful woman or a chariot or sensual friends. Think of the dejection he felt when the glamour of those things wore off and he realized what he gave up to have a few moments of fun and pleasure.

Picture trying to live on a quarter to a half of your paycheck after the divorce. Picture the poverty of your children trying to make it on only half of your salary. The quickest street to poverty is adultery and divorce. If there is barely enough money to go around now, there will a lot less if you give into adultery. You will also throw your children into poverty and emotional despair for a few stolen moments.

Visualize the devastation of picking up a disease: the AIDS virus or some other oozing and puss-producing sexual disease because you cannot control yourself. Picture the growing devastation in your family of sterility, pain, open sores, even death.

Picture abject loneliness: Loneliness is what results from trying to take the short cut to intimacy. Sex out of context is not intimacy, it is selfishness. Deep intimacy is about really caring for the other person and having them deeply care about you because they know you. The more time you pursue intimacy through the short cut, the lonelier your soul will be. See yourself sitting in a darkened room with no one who understands you and no one who really wants to listen to you, all everyone wants from you is money, time, and pleasure, but they do not want to really know you.

Picture members of your family watching you: I have talked with a number of men who have stated that the image of their mother or father or sister watching them engage in lustful behavior immediately brings them to a stop. This image of their family member watching them stops the ability to continue engaging in the lustful activity.

chapter sixteen

REMOVE SENSUAL FRIENDS AND SENSUAL ACTIVITIES

Remove Sensual Friends and Sensual Activities: 1 Cor. 15:33; Matt. 5:27, 28

I was talking with a young woman who said to me, "I have drawn my boundaries but I keep getting tempted to do stuff way past my boundaries." "Why is this happening?" I asked her whether she had friends who were doing things way past her boundaries. She said that she did. "But I don't do that stuff and they know that." I told her, "But the fact that you still hang out with them puts you in a place where they will tell you what they do." "The fact that you are around them puts you in a place where they can continually ask you to participate with them." I told her, "Until you are willing to move towards the Lord and away from these sensual friends, you will not have freedom from these temptations." She agreed and began moving away from these "friends" and allowing the Lord to pick new friends for her. This simple action brought a whole new freedom from lustful temptations in her life. She began living above the level of those temptations because she was not around the people who did those things. The Scriptures are clear, **"Bad company corrupts good morals."** (1 Cor. 15:33) We cannot hold out against the constant pressure of our friends tempting us to go beyond God's boundaries.

Many will argue and declare that loneliness is their only option if they move away from sensual friends. This is just not true. There are others who have not given in to sexual temptation, it only feels like everybody is doing it. However, if it takes loneliness for a period of time with the Lord Jesus as your only friend, then it is a blessing and you will be richer for the experience. God will find new friends for you if you will allow Him to deepen and refine you. Sometimes you do have to stop hanging out with the "cool" people, or you might have to seem a little backward, but it is worth it. You will be taking a real step forward in your ability to love people and learn how to build a great life.

Jesus says that if you have anything in your life which causes you to stumble, you need to get that out of your life no matter how precious it is to you.

> **Matt. 5:27-30 "You have heard that it was said, 'YOU SHALL NOT COMMIT ADULTERY'; but I say to you that everyone who looks at a woman with lust for her has already committed adultery with her in his heart. "If your right eye makes you stumble, tear it out and throw it from you; for it is better for you to lose one of the parts of your body, than for your whole body to be thrown into hell. "If your right hand makes you stumble, cut it off and throw it from you; for it is better for you to lose one of the parts of your body, than for your whole body to go into hell."**

If there is a friend or a group or an activity or a situation which always increases the temptation to be sensual or lustful, then have the courage to do what Jesus says and get that thing out of your life. It may be painful or difficult but it would be better to have a wounded former friend and have God be pleased than to have an evil friend be pleased with us and have God be displeased.

Spiritual Workout:
Eliminating Bad Company and Bad Activities

Do you have any friends who regularly violate God's standards? Who are they?

How can you move away from them?

This issue of moving away from friends who draw you into compromising situations is often very difficult. I believe that you must grapple with this area with your mentor or otherwise people, so that you will be ready for the push back and the clinginess that will surely come when you try to break away to a more temptation-free life. But let me give you some potential example strategies to use in moving away from bad activities and bad friends.

One of the most effective ways to eliminate wrong friends is to purposely move toward God and Godly activities. Invite your friends to come with your to Godly activities. Tell them that you are trying to move toward God. You are excited that they might want to come along as you pursue God. If the friends come with you then you have helped not only yourself but your friend. If they are unwilling to do the new activities that fill your life then it is them turning away from you, not you turning away from them.

Some people have prayed that God would take the wrong friends out of their life. If they are serious about this type of prayer, God may honor this request. I have watched God just blow a group of friends that were all wrong for each other. He may have some move. He may have some change jobs or schools. He may allow some to get into a quarrel. Again the point of this strategy is that you would care more about what God wants you to do than what your friends think. If you are not strong enough to handle the criticism or attack of your friends, God knows this and will often honor this type of request. But you cannot invite them back in your life once they are gone.

Sometimes God just wants you to take a stand and go public about your cutting from your old life. There are times when it is important to tell a person straight up that you can no longer hang with them. When they push back with, "Are you saying I am a bad influence?" The answer is "Yes, you are!" "And I become a bad influence when I am around you." "I am going to help you and help myself by not hanging around you so that we can both have the possibility of reaching our full potential." Often Christians have been taught that they don't want to offend people so we never share the truth or state the obvious. I know of young men and young women who were bold enough to state to their boyfriends or girlfriends, "You and I know that all we have is a physical attraction and while that is fun it is not a good thing, so we need to break up." We need more Christian young people with courage. If every time you are with a particular person the topic is sexual or the activity is sexual or the results of the interaction becomes sexual later, then it is a bad relationship and it needs to be cut off.

Another way to move away from wrong friends and wrong activities is crank up your work or activity schedule so that you do not have time for the wrong friends. This often involves substituting a new good friend and a new good activity for each wrong friend and wrong activity. You become too busy to hang around the wrong people any more. We often spend time with the wrong friends because we do not have anyone else to hang out with. Sometimes the substitution involves lots of work until the old friends have moved on and they do not expect you to be around.

Are there any people in your life that pressure you to go beyond God's boundaries sexually?

Who are they?

Are there activities or situations that always make you think about lust or sex?

What are they?

Are there any new people or groups of people that God seems to be directing you towards that you have not really checked out or gotten to know?

Who are they?

What would you have to do to connect with them?

Are there any new activities that God is directing your interest toward but you have not yet fully pursued?

What are they?

DIE TO LUST: PLAY DEAD AGAINST SEXUAL FANTASIES

Die to Lust: Play Dead Against Any Sexual Fantasy. Rom. 6:11-13

The truth of this powerful technique was demonstrated to me years ago as a teenager when an attractive young lady asked me if I wanted to go for a walk at a Christian camp. While we were way out away from other people she let me know that she liked me and was ready to interact with me in whatever way I desired. She then began touching me and holding me in ways I had not experienced before. If I had responded in the slightest to her advancements, lust would have won a huge victory. Just the few weeks before this incident my youth pastor had been training us how to apply Rom. 6:11-13. He taught us that we could die to lust and its urges and promptings, while still being alive. He showed us in Scripture where we could embrace our union with Christ in death and picture ourselves as dead to the temptation we were facing, and at the same time be alive to the actions that would praise God. By the grace of God, when this young lady began tempting me, I became a "Christian Zombie" to her advancements and suggestions. I was alive to God and what He wanted which seemed to be to move toward the main campgrounds, but I was a dead man walking. I am convinced that because I had memorized Rom. 6:11-13 and practiced playing dead to a number of lesser temptations, God thought I was ready for a big temptation. I did not respond to her advances or touches but kept slowly walking towards the main camp. In my mind I was thinking about an unresponsive dead corpse. I thought specifically about not moving my hands in response to her actions, because dead men do not respond. I repeated the words of Rom 6:11-13 over and over in my mind, **"Even so consider yourselves dead to sin but alive to God in Christ Jesus. Therefore do not let sin reign in your mortal body so that you obey its lusts, and do not go on presenting the members of your body to sin *as* instruments of unrighteousness; but present yourselves to God as those alive from the dead, and your members *as* instruments of righteousness to God."** I thought about pleasing God. The only way I could please God in that situation was to say little if anything and keep walking back toward the main camp while not responding. The urges and temptations that were coming at me were deflected by turning off or dying to that sexual aspect of my being. I am convinced that by the grace of God I was able to live to God while dying to fleshly temptations. When I got back to the other campers I knew that dying to lust was an extremely powerful weapon for defeating temptation. I have even thought about creating Christian Zombie T-shirts or Dead men walking T-shirts. Since that time God has proved over and over the power of dying to fleshly urges and living to His direction.

There are different responses to different types of temptations. Scripture consistently says that when you are faced with fleshly temptation you are to play dead or become unresponsive to that type of temptation (Rom. 6:11-13). When you are facing a Satanic temptation then you are to resist (Eph. 6:10-18). When you are facing a worldly temptation you are to not love it or let it love you (1 John 2:15-18). Scripture emphasizes that a key way to defeat fleshly temptations is to play dead to the mental images and fantasies that sin wants us to interact with. I am told that hunters are taught that if they are attacked by a bear and they cannot get away they should play dead. If they resist the bear it will tear you limb from limb, but if you play dead it will leave you alone, then you will have the chance to get away when the time is right. This is the same kind of idea in playing dead to lust when every fiber of your being wants to respond.

When a fleshly temptation rises within us, it is usually an emotional reaction or an image of what could happen. If instead of entering into a mental picture and seeing ourselves acting and reacting from within the mental storyline we just play dead, then temptation has nowhere to go with us. Instead of seeing ourselves cussing and swearing at the person who hurt us, we just see ourselves playing dead… not responding at all. If, instead of responding to, touching, looking and/or speaking to the sexually provocative woman, we play dead, not responding, then nothing will happen, and at the earliest possible moment get away from that temptation. If we do not respond then there will be no response. It is when we allow ourselves to be stirred up by temptation and interact with it and build on it that temptation has already won. It is only through dying to that mental or emotional scenario and living to a Godly scenario, that we can defeat temptation.

Years ago when my youth pastor taught us the truths of Romans 6:11 **"Even so consider yourselves dead to sin but alive to God in Christ Jesus. Therefore do not let sin reign in your mortal body so that you obey its lusts, and do not go on presenting the members of your body to sin *as* instruments of unrighteousness; but present yourselves to God as those alive from the dead, and your members *as* instruments of righteousness to God."** He taught us that if you picture yourself dead with your hands unable to move, your eyes unable to open, your mouth unable to speak, then a thousand naked women could march right over you and it would have no effect. So you must mentally see yourself as unified with Christ in death and no longer responding to the suggestions of sin, but instead respond only to the prompting of the Holy Spirit. This advice is hands-on practical, and will make a huge difference in the direction of people's lives if they will put these ideas into practice. The truths of Rom. 6:11-13 have proven to be especially helpful to people who are feeling an especially strong pull for temptation.

Let me add for the sake of balance, for those of you who are married that sexual fantasy has its place within marriage. A man or woman may enjoy sexual thoughts about their spouse. He/she should be the object of your sexual fantasy and fulfillment. The Scripture even suggests that your spouse's anatomy should please you at all times (Prov. 5:19). The only way to do this is through righteous marital fantasy. I have even suggested that some men take pictures of their wives in a swimsuit holding a wrench and put that in their tool box. Do not fantasize about sexual practices that would be beyond the boundaries of morality, even with your spouse. But enjoy the wonder of marriage with your spouse: spiritually, mentally, emotionally, and physically.

Spiritual Workout

Picture yourself as dead. This means seeing yourself as unable to move or respond in any way. Turn off your ability to respond sexually. Think about unresponsive behavior. (Most parents and teenagers know what this is like; whenever a parent asks a teen to do a chore the teen instinctively plays dead as though the parent didn't even say anything.)

Quote Rom. 6:11-13 to yourself until the power of the temptation passes.

Think about what would please God and slowly begin doing that.

Think through the temptations you faced last week and create a mental picture of you playing dead to one specific temptation at a time. No response from you at all. You have to be able to see yourself not responding to last weeks temptations or you will never respond correctly to this week's temptations. In the past you have allowed your body to respond to various stimuli in predictable ways. Now you are going to reprogram your body, emotions and mind to respond differently. You are renewing your mind with a Scriptural program for how to respond to various stimuli during the week. You will be playing dead to those internal lustful requests to respond. Other stimuli, mainly the prompting of the Holy Spirit, you will respond to with whole-hearted action.

Inside of this dead unresponsive body is an active mind asking God what you should do. As soon as God prompts you with a wholesome activity, energize your body to do that.

chapter eighteen

MAKE A COVENANT WITH YOUR EYES

Make a Covenant With Your Eyes: Job 31:1; Prov. 15:3

One of the key issues in winning the ongoing battle with lust is to be able to have control over where your eyes look. In our culture we tend to believe that our eyes are uncontrollable and will just look at whatever draws their attention. This is, however, not true. We can control what our eyes look at, especially over a long period of time. Advertisers and a host of media are trying to draw our attention to sensual images and ideas, but we can take control of this part of our body and choose to turn away. Let me give you an example: In Western culture privacy is the responsibility of those who want it. So we build fences, close doors, put up curtains, etc. In other parts of the world privacy is the responsibility of everyone so it is possible for a person to change on the side of the road and people will look away because they are respecting that person's privacy. It is possible to control what our eyes linger on, it is just not usually practiced in the West. Job says, **"I have made a covenant with my eyes, How then could I gaze at a virgin?"** Job had developed the habit of averting his eyes from staring at women. He had some kind of agreement with himself that he would look away.

Years ago when I was earning my way through graduate school I drove a delivery truck for a cola company. I discovered that in many stockrooms where I stacked the soda, the walls were covered with pornography. After a few days I made an agreement with another Christian delivery driver that we would look down at the floor rather than stare at the pornography covering the walls. We would check with each other at the end of each day to see if we had kept our promise to look down or away. This agreement and daily accountability significantly helped, and in a very short period of time proved that we could control where our eyes looked.

I remember working with a man who had the distracting habit of looking at a woman's body when he was talking to her, sweeping his eyes up and down her body and then focusing on one aspect of her body. This was completely inappropriate and derailed many professional and personal interactions with women. He had to get control over where his eyes looked. He needed to make his eyes focus on a woman's face and stay there the whole time that he talked to her. If he did not learn to do this then his career and social advancement would be significantly impacted. He made an agreement with his eyes that he would study a woman's face when he talked with her. Now some women dress so provocatively that it makes it a challenge to keep control over one's eyes; but it is essential that you direct your eyes rather than someone else, or have lust controlling where you look. It took him a while but he was able to learn to focus on a woman's face rather than let his eyes wander.

Many men need to think through where the visual triggers to lust are located in their life. In other words, they need to know what they were looking at right before they were attacked by temptation. It is these visual triggers that may seem innocent, but get a man thinking about lust or giving in to a sensual environment that creates the pathways for lust to win. When you understand what your visual triggers are, then you can make an agreement with your eyes and with another person to turn away from these triggers. Make sure that the person you talk to will hold you accountable. You have to know ahead of time where you will look when it is possible to stare at the visual trigger. This requires planning and training. It will take a while to train your eyes to look away. You will lose a few battles, but if you keep at it then you will learn to control your eyes. For some it is helpful if their accountability is automatic—by signing up to have every web site that you look at automatically sent to an accountability partner. This can be done through different computer programs. Covenant Eyes is one of these programs that I have recommended. (Covenant Eyes web site, *www.covenanteyes.com; www.x3.org;* Content Watch web site, *www.contentwatch.com*)

Spiritual Workout

Where in the past week have you looked that you probably shouldn't have?

During your typical week where are the visual enticements to lust?

Where could you look instead of looking at these temptations to lust?

Who could you enter into an accountability connection with to keep you honest?

Sign the following covenant and have an accountability partner and/or your spouse also sign it.

I, _____ declare that I will look away from pornography, sensual images, provocatively dressed people, and lustful information. I will no longer allow my eyes to look everywhere or to stare at tempting materials. I make an agreement with my eyes that they will divert to positive, wholesome, encouraging material. I will develop the control over where my eyes look. I will tell my accountability partner regularly where I fail and where I succeed in this agreement with my eyes.

Accountability partner _____

Accountability partner _____

chapter nineteen

MEDITATE ON KEY SCRIPTURES

Meditation on Key Scriptures: Psalm 119:10,11

For years I used to think that when the telephone repair men crawl down in the manholes and put out the little fan, that they were sucking the bad air out of the hole so that there would only be good air down where they were working. But I talked with a number of these men and they tell me there is so much bad air down the shaft that there is no way to suck it all out. The little fans are blowing good air down the hole and creating a pocket of good air for them to work in. These little fans push the bad air back with the good air so that there is an air space for them to work in. In a sense, this is exactly what you are doing when you meditate on the Scriptures. You are blowing the power of the Word of God into your soul so that you have a good spiritual space to live in. Without the constant good spiritual pressure of the Scriptures in your life, you would be overcome by the toxic fumes of temptations.

I have to be honest that this material in this chapter is the most powerful technique I have ever seen in giving men and women victory over temptation. The greatest progress is made when people get serious about meditating on Scripture. God promises all kinds of blessings in your life if you will meditate upon His word (Joshua 1:8; Ps. 1:1-3; Col. 3:16). I have watched men who have been addicted to pornography or visiting prostitutes begin meditating on Scripture, memorizing it, and letting it run through their minds constantly, and the power of the addiction is broken.

I remember one conversation with a young man who was addicted to pornography and had numerous affairs. He said, "I am amazed at how clear my mind is of the sexual thoughts." "As long as I mediate on the Scriptures I am fine, but if I stop quoting Scriptures and going through the other ways of meditating on the Bible then I can literally feel the temptations flowing back into my life."

There is incredible power in the Word of God to reorder our thinking and energize new actions, if it is memorized and meditated upon. God promises all kinds of benefits to those who would take the time to work on meditating on the Scriptures (Joshua 1:8; Ps. 1:1-3; Ps. 119:10, 11; Col. 3:16). The Scripture is powerful enough if its suggestions are mentally embraced to drive out other thoughts and develop new actions.

Using various methods for meditation will imprint the Scriptures into your soul and spirit. It will allow you to overcome lust and truly seek to love others in your life. The following methods of Biblical meditation can be used on various Scripture passages that deal directly or indirectly with purity, love and lust:

Slow Repetition: Slowly repeat a Scripture out loud. Read it or say it from memory about ten times slowly. You are not in a hurry. Emphasize different words and parts of verses as you go over it each time. As you speak out the verse, ask God to give you insight into how it applies to you. The process of saying Scripture slowly allows the Scripture to be imbedded in your soul.

Study: This is where you set about studying a passage of Scripture. There are three classic steps of Bible Study: Observation, Interpretation and Application. *Observation* means carefully observing the passage. Here is how you might do that: Reading the passage at least three times; write out the passage on a separate page; notice and circle key words; write out questions that arise from taking careful note of the passage. *Interpretation* is the next part of Bible Study and means trying to accurately understand what the author meant by what they wrote. *Interpretation* involves: defining key words in a dictionary; understanding any background or historical material which impacts the verse; answering the various questions that you have asked about the verse(s); writing your own paraphrase version of the verse(s). *Application* is the third part of the Bible Study process. Application involves: Answering: What does God want me to know, feel or do with the information in this verse; how does this apply to my life; why do I need to know this information today.

Memorize: A forgotten but crucial discipline for getting Scripture in your soul. If you will slowly read a Scripture out loud ten times, you will usually find that you can say it from memory. When you can say it five times without looking it is memorized, and you have it with you all the time.

Personalize: This is where you insert your name and/or your problems into the verse, writing the verse specifically for you. It is very helpful to write or type out a verse inserting your name or personal pronouns into the verse to "personalize" the verse for you.

Confessionalize: This is the process where you confess what is in the passage. If it is a truth, then you agree with God about that; if it is a command that you have kept, then agree with God about that; if the verse points out something that you haven't done, then you agree with God about that. This Biblical meditation technique pushes the Scripture through your will.

Visualize: This is the process of picturing what the Scripture would look like. You can picture a Biblical story or you can picture what you would look like doing the Biblical truth. This type of meditation is extremely powerful. Creating a movie of what you will look like doing righteousness allows the mind and body to get used to living God's way. If you cannot see yourself doing the right thing ahead of time, you will not do it. So "pre-see" yourself living out Scripture.

Pray: This is where you pray about everything in the verse. This could mean that you praise God for the truths that are mentioned. This could mean that you ask God for grace and power to live out the verse. This could mean that you would ask God to help other people who are struggling with the issues mentioned in the verse. This could mean that you would cry out to God for wisdom about what is mentioned in the verse. The main thing is that you interact with God over the contents of that Scripture.

Sing: This is where you sing the Scriptures or listen to Scripture songs. It can be extremely enlightening and helpful to sing the verse of Scripture that you are meditating upon. You can use any tune just begin singing. It will feel a little funny at first but it will really open up your soul. You could sing the exact words of Scripture and adjust the tune to match. You could sing a paraphrased version of the verse. You could sing about a truth, insight or feeling that is talked about in the verse. You may want to do this in a more private place so that you feel more relaxed.

Diagram: This is where you draw a schematic of the verse, or pictures of the truths in the verse. It can be very helpful to actually draw out a schematic of what is happening in the verse, or what is supposed to be happening in your life. All of a sudden you can see it. Drawing pictures of the truths in a verse can also give you a different picture of the truths, and connect these truths more deeply with your emotions.

If you would like to see a fuller discussion of Biblical meditation techniques, please see Dr. Gil's book: ***Spiritual Disciplines of a C.H.R.I.S.T.I.A.N.***

The greatest weapon that God has given you in your war against sin and temptation is Scripture. It is an offensive weapon. It is a defensive weapon. It is a strategic planning weapon. If you are willing to draw Scripture into your soul and act upon, it will place you in the land of purity with a different life than is possible if you give in to the gutter life of sexual temptation and license. It may seem like a lot of work to meditate on the Scripture, but it is worth it. Just as the players on a football team study the playbook and practice the plays so they can win in the game, so a Christian man needs to study the playbook and practice the plays of righteousness so they can win at the game of life. Man after man has told me that when they are meditating on Scripture it blows back the pollution of the world and allows them to break free from the pull of lust.

Spiritual Workout:

Meditation on God's Word

The following verses need to be an internal part of the way you think. That only will happen if you practice the various Biblical methods of meditation on the Scripture. Do not just look at the verses listed and tell yourself, "Those are great Scriptures and would really help." You must actually push through meditating on these Scriptures if you are going to break the power of lust in you life. Get in a small group or have an accountability partner who would be willing to read or listen to your insights on these Scriptures, once you have meditated on them. I cannot emphasize enough the power of the Word of God if it is meditated on. Each verse that is listed needs to be meditated upon. I have personally witnessed men who never thought they could beat back their addictive interest in pornography or sex become victorious because of this exercise. I had one man say to me, "As long as I meditate on these Scriptures, I am fine. But if I don't, then the power of sexual temptation pours right back into my life." Put a check mark by the meditation technique when you have completed it over a Scripture. Only check the verse itself when you have finished all the various techniques for that verse.

Verses for Scriptural Meditation

1 Cor. 3:13 "Each man's work will become evident; for the day will show it because it is *to be* revealed with fire, and the fire itself will test the quality of each man's work."

o Slow Repetition: o Visualize:

o Study: o Pray:

o Memorize: o Sing:

o Personalize: o Diagram:

o Confessionalize:

2 Cor. 10:3-5 "For though we walk in the flesh, we do not war according to the flesh, for the weapons of our warfare are not of the flesh, but divinely powerful for the destruction of

fortresses. *We are* destroying speculations and every lofty thing raised up against the knowledge of God, and *we are* taking every thought captive to the obedience of Christ."

o Slow Repetition: o Visualize:
o Study: o Pray:
o Memorize: o Sing:
o Personalize: o Diagram:
o Confessionalize:

James 1:2-4 "Consider it all joy, my brethren, when you encounter various trials, knowing that the testing of your faith produces endurance. And let endurance have *its* perfect result, so that you may be perfect and complete, lacking in nothing."

o Slow Repetition: o Visualize:
o Study: o Pray:
o Memorize: o Sing:
o Personalize: o Diagram:
o Confessionalize:

1 Thess. 4:3-5 "For this is the will of God, your sanctification; *that is,* that you abstain from sexual immorality; that each of you know how to possess his own vessel in sanctification and honor, not in lustful passion, like the Gentiles who do not know God."

o Slow Repetition: o Visualize:
o Study: o Pray:
o Memorize: o Sing:
o Personalize: o Diagram:
o Confessionalize:

Rom. 6:11-13 "Even so consider yourselves dead to sin but alive to God in Christ Jesus. Therefore do not let sin reign in your mortal body so that you obey its lusts, and do not go on presenting the members of your body to sin *as* instruments of unrighteousness; but present yourselves to God as those alive from the dead, and your members *as* instruments of righteousness to God."

o Slow Repetition: o Visualize:
o Study: o Pray:
o Memorize: o Sing:
o Personalize: o Diagram:
o Confessionalize:

Gal. 5:16 "But I say, walk by the Spirit, and you will not carry out the desire of the flesh."

o Slow Repetition: o Visualize:
o Study: o Pray:
o Memorize: o Sing:
o Personalize: o Diagram:
o Confessionalize:

Gal. 5:22, 23 "But the fruit of the Spirit is love, joy, peace, patience, kindness, goodness, faithfulness, gentleness, self-control; against such things there is no law."

o Slow Repetition: o Visualize:
o Study: o Pray:
o Memorize: o Sing:
o Personalize: o Diagram:
o Confessionalize:

Gal. 5:24 "Now those who belong to Christ Jesus have crucified the flesh with its passions and desires."

o Slow Repetition: o Visualize:
o Study: o Pray:
o Memorize: o Sing:
o Personalize: o Diagram:
o Confessionalize:

Col. 3:2, 5 "Set your mind on the things above, not on the things that are on earth. Therefore consider the members of your earthly body as dead to immorality, impurity, passion, evil desire, and greed, which amounts to idolatry."

o Slow Repetition: o Visualize:
o Study: o Pray:
o Memorize: o Sing:
o Personalize: o Diagram:
o Confessionalize:

Heb. 12:11, 12 "All discipline for the moment seems not to be joyful, but sorrowful; yet to those who have been trained by it, afterwards it yields the peaceful fruit of righteousness. Therefore, strengthen the hands that are weak and the knees that are feeble."

o Slow Repetition: o Visualize:
o Study: o Pray:
o Memorize: o Sing:
o Personalize: o Diagram:
o Confessionalize:

Ps. 1:1-3 "How blessed is the man who does not walk in the counsel of the wicked, Nor stand in the path of sinners, Nor sit in the seat of scoffers! But his delight is in the law of the LORD, and in His law he meditates day and night. He will be like a tree *firmly* planted by streams of water, which yields its fruit in its season and its leaf does not wither; and in whatever he does, he prospers."

o Slow Repetition: o Visualize:
o Study: o Pray:
o Memorize: o Sing:
o Personalize: o Diagram:
o Confessionalize:

Ps. 19:14 "Let the words of my mouth and the meditation of my heart be acceptable in Your sight, O LORD, my rock and my Redeemer."

- o Slow Repetition:
- o Study:
- o Memorize:
- o Personalize:
- o Confessionalize:
- o Visualize:
- o Pray:
- o Sing:
- o Diagram:

Ps. 119:9, 11 "How can a young man keep his way pure? By keeping *it* according to Your word. Your word I have treasured in my heart, That I may not sin against You."

- o Slow Repetition:
- o Study:
- o Memorize:
- o Personalize:
- o Confessionalize:
- o Visualize:
- o Pray:
- o Sing:
- o Diagram:

Judges 16:21 "Then the Philistines seized him and gouged out his eyes; and they brought him down to Gaza and bound him with bronze chains, and he was a grinder in the prison."

- o Slow Repetition:
- o Study:
- o Memorize:
- o Personalize:
- o Confessionalize:
- o Visualize:
- o Pray:
- o Sing:
- o Diagram:

Job 31:1 "I have made a covenant with my eyes, How then could I gaze at a virgin?"

- o Slow Repetition:
- o Study:
- o Memorize:
- o Personalize:
- o Confessionalize:
- o Visualize:
- o Pray:
- o Sing:
- o Diagram:

Prov. 15:3 "The eyes of the Lord are in every place, Watching the evil and the good."

- o Slow Repetition:
- o Visualize:

- o Study:
- o Pray:
- o Memorize:
- o Sing:
- o Personalize:
- o Diagram:
- o Confessionalize:

Rom. 12:1, 2 "Therefore I urge you, brethren, by the mercies of God, to present your bodies a living and holy sacrifice, acceptable to God, *which is* your spiritual service of worship. And do not be conformed to this world, but be transformed by the renewing of your mind, so that you may prove what the will of God is, that which is good and acceptable and perfect."

- o Slow Repetition:
- o Visualize:
- o Study:
- o Pray:
- o Memorize:
- o Sing:
- o Personalize:
- o Diagram:
- o Confessionalize:

chapter twenty

TREAT TEMPTATION LIKE A SET OF WAVES

Treat temptation like a set of waves: James 1:14

It can be helpful to think of temptation as a powerful wave wanting to carry you away from where you should be. The Apostle James has this kind of idea when he says, **"But each one is tempted when he is carried away and enticed by his own lust."** Lust is a very powerful wave of desire, emotion and/or promise that seeks to move you off of your normal life and have you floating along with its dictates. Lust will build in its power as you resist it, but that doesn't mean you are loosing. It is the normal course of temptation.

Too often people give in to lust right when they are about to win. The pressure to give in gets stronger and stronger, and then it lets up. When you are at the ocean and you see a huge wave coming that is too big for you to handle, you get out of the water or dive under the wave and let it pass over you. Either way you should not let the power of the wave hit you. I have listened to some men say that they wanted to build themselves up to the point where they could stand in a room full of alluring women and not give in to lust. This is ridiculous. If the waves are too big, get out of the water or dive under the wave so you aren't exposed to the full power of it. Realize that given the right circumstance almost everyone would give in.

How do you dive under the power of a wave of temptation? ***Quote Scripture until it passes.*** You will find yourself at various times in situations where you can't flee and lust is growing in strength. At those times start quoting Scripture until the power of the temptation passes. Almost any Scripture will do but it can be very helpful to quote Scripture that is about purity or righteousness or resisting sin. I recommend that you be prepared to just under your breath or very loudly quote Scripture until the power of the temptation passes. Many times folks have never really realized the build up, power and back side of temptation. It can be very helpful to realize that temptation is not eternal nor omnipresent, nor omnipotent… it has a beginning, middle and an end. Temptation also tends to come in sets of waves just like the ocean. Three sets of waves and then a 5-set wave pattern. If you can understand that this is a pattern that you do not have to be driven by, but can get around the power of the temptation, it can be very helpful.

Spiritual Workout

FITNESS

Take a deep breath in and slowly repeat one of the Scriptures you have memorized as you breathe out. Keep repeating the verse slowly until the power of the temptation has passed. The verse can be said under your breath with your lips barely moving, but it is important to physically say the verse to engage the whole person. Practice doing this so that you can do it when lust is rising in you and you cannot flee.

Suggested Scriptures: 1 Thess. 4:3-5; Prov. 15:3; Ps. 1:1; 1 Cor. 10:13; Phil. 4:7,8; 1 Cor. 6:18; James 1:14; Gal. 5:16; Gal. 6:7; 2 Tim. 2:22

chapter twenty-one

GET SERIOUS ABOUT RESISTING SIN

Get Serious About Resisting Sin: Heb. 12:4

Heb. 12:4 says, **"You have not yet resisted to the point of shedding blood in your striving against sin."** In the early church, Christians had to be willing to be martyred rather than to commit sin. Some Christians in Jerusalem were unwilling to fight to stay pure and undefiled before the Lord. The price for purity was high. The writer of the book of Hebrews is right that fighting to not sin will cost a heavy price at times. Sometimes we are not willing to pay the price. We want it to be easy to avoid sin. It doesn't seem right that we have to fight to not sin. How far are you willing to go to resist sinning? Do you see this struggle against lust as important enough to have it really cost you if you don't succeed? I want to give a different twist on applying this verse of Scripture to your life. I have helped a number of people turn away from particular sins. Sometimes voluntary negative reinforcement can be an effective tool in helping people turn away from sin. In other words, if you agree that should you give in to a particular sin you will do a very distasteful chore, or you will write out a verse 100 times, or you will give someone a hundred dollars, or some other negative action. Negative reinforcement can be over used and should never be involuntarily applied, but it can act as a strong motivator and reminder to not give in. For some of us the only thing that motivates us is the fear of loss. If this is true then we need to get some of the fear of loss working in our favor. Work out with your accountability group what losses or negative reinforcements would be strong enough that it would make you think twice before you gave in again.

I can remember talking to one young man who was really struggling with pornography. He assured me that he wanted to break the pornography habit, and we had spent time confessing and praying and trying to install the right measures to help him. I then asked him if he was going with a particular young lady in the church. He said that he was and that he liked her very much. I then raised the price of sin for him and it helped immeasurably. I told him that if I heard or in any way found out that he had given into this pornography problem, I would assign his girlfriend's father to be his accountability partner on this issue. This young man had a whole new level of resolve to resist this sin.

On another issue, but related to the topic of raising the price of sin, I was asked by a man to help him stop cursing. He told me that it was a real problem for him and he knew he needed to stop. His family was standing around him and agreed that he had a problem. I let him know that I potentially had something that would most likely cure the habit of cursing and swearing quickly. He said that he was very interested in doing it. I told him that if he was willing to give each of his two boys 10 dollars every time they heard a curse word come out of his mouth, he would learn to control his tongue quickly. His boys looked at each other as if to say we will be rich. While he agreed that it would work, he said that my solution was too extreme and he did not want to try it.

Spiritual Workout

What consequences would be severe enough to cause you stop giving in to lust?

> Public exposure:
> Writing out a Scripture verse a hundred times
> Computer reporting or tracking software installed
> Computer seizure:
> 5 – 10 – 20 – 50 -100 dollar fines
> A new accountability partner
> Confess to spouse or boss or friend
> Counseling:
> Chores:
> No favorite hobby for a week or a month
> Etc.

chapter twenty-two

CELEBRATE YOUR VICTORIES

Celebrate Your Victories Phil. 3:1; Eph. 5:5-8

Many Christians do not celebrate their victories. We often see a victory as what we were supposed to do anyway so why make a big deal out it. We see everything from the perspective of the unprofitable servant. Luke 17:10, **"Even so ye also, when ye shall have done all the things that are commanded you, say, We are unprofitable servants; we have done that which it was our duty to do."** But there are significant reasons to celebrate our victories even when they may be minor and seemingly insignificant. When we do not rejoice, reward and celebrate our victories, we have less motivation for repeating the good behavior. I have asked numerous people what they do to celebrate when they win a victory over a lustful temptation. They have no idea what I am talking about or they don't know how to celebrate without allowing it to become sinful.

We need a significant way of saying that we won a victory. How do we reward ourselves when: we did not pick up the pornography; we did not flirt with the woman; we did not enter into the mental fantasy world, we did not make the crude remark; we did not watch the sensual movie; we did not touch the office worker; we did not stare at the woman with the revealing dress; we did not visit the porn web site; we did look to minister to our wives instead of taking; we did study floors, doors and other non-sexual things; we did play dead when temptation started to speak to us; we did quote Scripture until the power of the temptation passed by, etc. All of these and much more positive steps call for at least small celebrations and rejoicing in order to reinforce that we are on the right road. Too often we beat ourselves up over how close we came to giving in, instead of congratulating ourselves for the fact that we turned away.

Listen to Eph. 5:8,9 and its advice about enjoying the fruit of walking in the Light. Listen for the celebration of what is good. Listen for the enjoyment of righteousness. **"Therefore do not be partakers with them; for you were formerly darkness, but now you are Light in the Lord; walk as children of Light (for the fruit of the Light _consists_ in all goodness and righteousness and truth)."** Don't you hear the celebration in this verse. God has given believers the best of the world and we should revel in His goodness. When we are trying to break an attachment to what is wrong we need to substitute the bad behavior with something really good. The Christian can have fun without the guilt, shame and hangover afterwards. It is this kind of good clean fun that you must inject into your life if you are to have a real hope of overcoming destructive desires. If you are not careful it will seem like the unbelievers are having all the fun and all you get to do is say no to yourself.

Christians need to remind themselves of the truth that God created and gives all kinds of good things that we are to enjoy. James 1:17, **"Every good thing given and every perfect gift is from above, coming down from the Father of lights, with whom there is no variation or shifting shadow."** When we stay away from destructive desires it does not mean that we must drain all the good and rewarding things from our life. In fact, if we are going to stay pure we must make sure that we have a deeply fulfilling and enjoyable life.

It is interesting that the Apostle Paul says that those who come with the doctrine of demons will be those who have all kinds of regulations and requirements about what you cannot do. They will tell you that you can't get married, they will tell you that you can't have feasts and certain foods. Those who are peddling the enemy's message will be those who do not know how to have a righteous good time. 1 Tim. 4:1-5, **"But the Spirit explicitly says that in later times some will fall away from the faith, paying attention to deceitful spirits and doctrines of demons, by means of the hypocrisy of liars seared in their own conscience as with a branding iron,** *men* **who forbid marriage** *and advocate* **abstaining from foods which God has created to be gratefully shared in by those who believe and know the truth. For everything created by God is good, and nothing is to be rejected if it is received with gratitude; for it is sanctified by means of the word of God and prayer."** One of the hazards of living a religious life is the religious people who enjoy being negative and pessimistic. They seek to inject into every Christian group their negativity and enjoyment of pessimism. They will try to steal your joy. "Are you enjoying that?" they will ask. "Stop it." "You are having too much fun," they will declare.

It is important that when you are beginning to make a change in battle with destructive desires that you reward yourself every time you turn away from the wrong desire and do the good, righteous and noble thing. It must pay to do the right thing. There are all kinds of these rewards like going to a ball game, buying a book, having a desert, buying something you wanted, romantic time with your wife, vacation, etc.

Spiritual Workout

Make a list of 10 wholesome activities that you really enjoy.

1.
2.
3.
4.
5.
6.
7.
8.
9.
10.

Make a list of 10 wholesome activities that you would like to try.

1.
2.
3.
4.
5.
6.
7.
8.
9.
10.

What little rewards can you use to stay motivated to not give in?
If I get to the end of the day without giving in, I will…

chapter twenty-three

PREPARE FOR WEAK TIMES

Prepare for Weak Times: Heb. 12:12

There may be times in your battle against destructive desires when you will want to give in and you will want a wrong desire to win. You must prepare for those times of weakness so that you cannot give in at those times. You must build fences, boundaries, guard rails so that it is virtually impossible to give in to a destructive desire. Just as we would put up barbed wire and barricades to repel an invading enemy, so we must erect barriers to our involvement in sin. We put up fences to keep children from running into the streets by accident. In the same ways you must prepare for when lust makes assault on your life. There may be certain times of the day when you are most susceptible to lust. There may be certain situations which make you more pliable to lust's suggestions. There may be certain people or certain places which regularly move you in the direction of lust. Barriers, boundaries and barricades must be installed to keep you from giving in at those times. These boundaries are rules of conduct, lack of access, penalties, accountabilities, etc, anything that will effectively stop us from crossing the line and giving in to a destructive desire.

Scripture is clear in Heb. 12:12, **"Therefore, strengthen the**

hands that are weak and the knees that are feeble." There will be times when you are not strong enough to resist temptation. You need to be strengthened with an outside form. The example in Scripture is of a splint or cast that makes a broken bone stay straight. God knows that there will be times when you are so weak that you will not be able to resist temptation and you will need help. There will be specific situations, types of temptation, particular circumstances where you will give in if you have not prepared ahead of time and if you do not have the help of others. We must stop kidding ourselves, there are types of sins that we in ourselves offer little or no resistance against.

Let me give you a few examples. Ralph found that he consistently gave in to pornography on the computer after 10 p.m. so he made a rule with his wife that he would not be on the computer after 10 p.m. Jim found that when he went on business trips the other men would always end up at a strip club after dinner together, so he made a rule to eat at the hotel restaurant so he would not be with them when they inevitably went to a strip club. Dave found that pornographic shows on television were a major temptation so he always instructs the hotel desk clerk before he goes to the room to turn off those options. Rich made a pact with his wife to not view the television at all when away on business trips. Gene found that driving a particular way home took him past adult bookstores and strip clubs that were too tempting, so he took a longer but temptation-free way home. Andy found that every time he was alone with his girlfriend at his apartment, they were tempted to go too far so he asked another Christian brother to be present and not leave when he and his girlfriend were present. Rob was tempted by the Internet but found that when he installed filters and software that recorded every web site he visited and mailed it to his accountability partners, he was strengthened to not give in. John found that every time he spent time with a certain friend it often involved pornography or strip clubs and the like, so he eliminated time with that friend.

Spiritual Workout:

What guard rails do you have to put in place?
Television:
Travel:
Friends:
Computer:
Magazines:
Mail:
Phone:
Accountability:
Physical Touch:
Other:

What guard rails do you need to put in place?
Television:
Travel:
Friends:
Computer:
Magazines:
Mail:
Phone:
Accountability:
Physical Touch:
Other:

chapter twenty-four

JOIN AN ACCOUNTABILITY GROUP

Join an Accountability Group or Structure: James 5:16

Every time nations, churches and individuals have been revived in their faith it has been partially due to their willingness to be accountable to others for the practice of their faith. No one can be a Lone Ranger Christian for long. James 5:16 says, **"Therefore, confess your sins to one another, and pray for one another so that you may be healed. The effective prayer of a righteous man can accomplish much."** We need to have those who are more mature than ourselves that will keep us moving toward the goal of becoming more Christ-like. We all need others to help us keep fighting the good fight of faith. In the early church people met in house groups to hear and be held accountable for their practice of the Christian life. In the Methodist revivals of the 1700's John Wesley organized weekly classes which encouraged, taught and corrected people in their pursuit of godliness. It is best to find a group of respected individuals who can help you remain revived in your faith. They should be given the right to ask you a set of questions weekly or monthly about this crucial area of purity. Here is a list of suggested questions that they might ask:

- What spiritual disciplines did you practice this last week?
- What temptations have you successfully resisted in the last week?
- What temptations have you struggled with in the last week?
- What do you hear the Holy Spirit say to you when you are being tempted?
- Do you have any secret ways to indulge in destructive desires?
- How can I help you win against destructive desires?

Fred came to see me about his problem with pornography and masturbation. He was a young single Christian man struggling with the destructive desires that kept bubbling up in this area. I met with him and walked him through a process of confession and restoration. I assigned him to begin meditating on Scripture and doing a number of the practical spiritual exercises in this book. He began making progress and was doing much better in his battle with lust, even though he did stumble a few times as he was moving forward. After one of his difficult periods when he had given in and indulged in some pornographic material, I shocked him by saying that I was going to help him get serious. He assured me that he was serious and wanted to really get a handle on love and not giving in to selfish desires. I ask him if he was dating a young lady in our church. He replied that he was and that enjoyed that relationship very much. I let him know that if he returned to pornography one more time I would tell this young lady's father and I would ask him to be his accountability partner in his battle against pornography. He made significant progress after that meeting and did not return to pornography.

I have noticed that many young men are being significantly helped by computer programs that send an e-mail of every place they visit on the web to designated people. (e.g. *www.covenatneyes.com, www.x3.org, www.contentwatch.com*) For the first time they have an accountability partner with some real knowledge. They can no longer hide what they are doing, so they stop.

I was working with one young man, Kevin, years ago and he was struggling with pornography and his incredible thirst for it. One of the things that I did in working with him, in order to take his commitment to the next level, was to ask his finance to become his accountability partner and help her understand the level of his attraction and embracing of this material. He made a huge leap forward in his ability to resist this material because she was now involved. The point is that whoever and however you inject a level of accountability into your life, it must have some teeth in it. Accountability does no good if the people you are telling do not get the straight story or you do not respect them enough to stop.

FITNESS

Spiritual Workout:

The following are projects to increase the level of accountability in your life. A lack of accountability and the feeling of "no one will know" provides fertile ground for destructive desires to grow. Become part of a small group which will hold you accountable and encourage you with questions like this:

Relationship With God:

What spiritual disciplines did you practice this last week?

Which of the 3 enemies of the faith is bothering you most? World, Flesh, Devil

What are the World, Flesh and Devil trying to do to you?

Self:

How are you developing your self?

Are you struggling with any of the 7 deadly sins more than others?

(Pride, Envy, Anger, Lust, Sloth, Gluttony, Greed)

Marriage:

Which of your spouse's needs did you meet this week?

What ways did you meet your spouses needs this last week?

Did you have any SAD (selfish, angry, destructive) behaviors this week?

Family:

What did you do this week to fulfill the 4 R's in your family?

Which of the R's needs work?

Work:

Which of the 8 skills of a great worker did you practice this week?

Which of the 8 key skills did you fail to demonstrate at work this week?

What and/or who are your major enemies at work?

Church:

Are you involved in corporate WDEFC (Worship, Discipleship, Evangelism, Fellowship, Compassion)?

Did you participate in the 5 purposes of the church this last week? WDEFC

What keeps you being involved in a corporate expression of your faith?

Finances

Are you keeping a good balance of Income, Management, Giving?
What is the major enemy of your financial health?

Society:

How are you involved in helping your society? Recovery, Prevention, Justice

Which of the 10 commandments are you noticing being most attacked?

Friends:

Are you maintaining friends at each of the levels?
What is the top two enemies of friendship this week?

Enemies:

Did you get a chance to love, bless, pray or go the second mile for an enemy this week?

Did you make an enemy *more* of an enemy this week?

Rate your 10 Major Relationships
on a scale of 1-10
1 being bad and 10 being perfect

God	Self	Marriage/ Dating	Family	Work	Church	$	Society	Friends	Enemies
⇕	⇕	⇕	⇕	⇕	⇕	⇕	⇕	⇕	⇕

Rate how each relationship is at the moment.

Rate whether that relationship is improving or declining.

Provide your small group with actual consequences that they can implement in your life if you do not win in this battle. Giving in to sin must cost you or you will not hold back. Add a computer program to your computer that will send a list of every web page that you visit to three different people.

chapter twenty-five

TRANSFER THE BATTLE TO AN ARENA YOU CAN WIN

Transfer the Battle to an Arena in Which You Can Win: Matt. 17:21

If you are in a time of great sexual temptation or have given in significantly to lust, then the battleground may need to change. The most Scriptural way to change the battleground is fasting. Skip a day of eating and pray and read the Word during your normal eating periods. After a few skipped meals you will only be thinking about eating not lustful images. At times God may call you to a longer fast of three days or more in order to break the hold of a particular temptation.

Scripture records that most giants of the faith used fasting to increase the power of prayer, to draw near to God, and to get clarity about what they should do in times of uncertainty. In Matt. 4:2 Jesus was led up into the wilderness to be tempted, and He fasted and prayed for forty days. Jesus himself said that a certain kind of demonic stronghold would not be broken unless there had been a sufficient amount of fasting and prayer about the problem (Matt. 17:21). In Nehemiah 9:1, 2 the governor Nehemiah had all the people fast and confess their sins in order to bring God's blessing and forgiveness upon the people. In Matt. 6:16, Jesus give a discourse on fasting suggesting that it should be regular, hidden, and directed toward God. **"Whenever you fast, do not put on a gloomy face as the hypocrites *do*, for they neglect their appearance so that they will be noticed by men when they are fasting. Truly I say to you, they have their reward in full."** Daniel wanted to understand the work of God in the world, and set upon an extended fast to seek the Lord's face and wisdom (Dan. 9:3). Fasting is a weapon in the continuing battle against temptation.

Tracy was struggling with a significant amount of lustful thoughts toward his girlfriend. I suggested that he go on an extended fast to focus on God and seek His direction for certain decisions in His life. It was very difficult to get started but he did fast for three days over a weekend. He prayed, sang, walked, worshipped, read and generally focused on the Lord during this spiritual retreat without food. The extended fast broke the power of his lustful focus on his girlfriend. He was able to spend time with this young woman without being bombarded by temptation. His increased focus on the Lord also allowed him to follow His leading to college rather than just pursue this young woman.

Three young men who were struggling greatly under the power of sexual temptation ask me if I could help them win against the power of temptation. I recommended that they go on a three-day spiritual retreat, spending time fasting, praying, worshipping, confessing their sins, reading spiritual books, hiking, encouraging one another, and other spiritual disciplines. They went on a Friday, Saturday, and Sunday morning retreat, and it proved to be an extremely powerful tool in letting them put the Lord back in charge rather than lust.

Fasting and other abstinence disciplines can be very effective in battling fleshly temptations and refocusing your attention on God. Moses, David, Hannah, Daniel, Jesus, Paul, and many other Godly people used fasting to beat back temptation and draw them near to God. Please refer to my book *Spiritual Disciplines of a C.H.R.I.S.T.I.A.N.* and the section on fasting for more details about how to fast and its benefits and dangers. Drink a lot of water and let every prompt to eat be a prompt to pray. God can work powerfully in our lives when we learn to say no to our fleshly urges and yes to Him.

Now it is true that certain periods of the church have gone

overboard using disciplines of abstinence. Even the Apostle Paul in the book of Colossians says to beware of overuse of this discipline. The fact that it has been overused should not keep us from using it properly. This discipline can be effectively used in our battle with temptation and sin.

Spiritual Workout

Plan a one-meal fast and spiritual retreat:

Plan on skipping one meal this next week in order to pursue the Lord and to let your body know that it does not always get what it wants. Fasting is a way of saying that spiritual things trump physical things. This could be in the middle of the work day or in the evening or on a weekend. Set aside the hour you would have been eating for praying, confessing, memorizing, meditating, studying the Bible, and worshipping.

Many times this one-meal fast and spiritual retreat is a way to begin a deeper seeking of the Lord. It may not seem like much but setting aside one day's meals to seek the Lord and pursue the holy life is very significant. The pressures of modern life do not always allow as many "perfect" long spiritual retreats as we would like, but these small "mini" retreats are a great escape from the insanity of modern life. Often just a prayer list and your Bible will fill the whole hour. Don't feel guilty that it was not longer, enjoy the time seeking God.

Plan a two-meal fast and spiritual retreat:

This type of two-meal fast and spiritual retreat is often a way to fast for a 24 hour period. Eat a good meal the night before but do not eat anything after the meal. Every time you are prompted to eat something use that as a prompt to pray. The next morning skip breakfast and use the time to pray, worship, read your Bible and seek the Lord. Then go about your normal day. When it is time for lunch do not eat, but again spend the time seeking the Lord through prayer, worship, Bible study, Biblical meditation. Then when it is time for the evening meal, go ahead and eat. Then come to a prayer meeting with other Christians so that you can finish off your mini spiritual retreat. It is often a great encouragement to seek the Lord together with others after a fast.

This type of two-meal fast can be just a simple solo fast for the sake of seeking the Lord in the middle of the week, without the evening before or the prayer meeting in the evening. Just skip breakfast and lunch or lunch and dinner to focus time on the Lord. In whatever way seems appropriate.

Plan a 3-Day Spiritual Retreat:

Plan a Spiritual Retreat in which you will fast and seek God's face for three days. Usually these type of retreats last Friday night, all day Saturday and then Sunday until about noon. This seems to fit best with a modern schedule. These retreats can be with other like-minded people or it could be done solo. It is best to get away from your normal surroundings and go somewhere else. There are plenty of retreat centers around or you could just rent a motel room for three days, or stay at a friend's cabin or apartment if you will be allowed to pursue a more spiritual schedule. Bring your Bible and other books that will allow you to focus on the Lord. Books that have proven helpful are Christian Classics like: *God's Chosen Fast* by Arthur Wallis; *Knowledge of the Holy* by A.W. Tozer; *Knowing God* by J.I. Packer; *The Christian Secret to a Happy Life* by Hannah Whitall Smith; *With Christ in the School of Prayer* by Andrew Murray, etc. There are multitudes of great Christian books that can encourage you while in the midst of a spiritual retreat. Plan to do a number of Spiritual Disciplines over the time of the retreat: Confession, Listening at a new level to the Holy Spirit's promptings, Bible Study, Meditation on Scripture, Worship, etc. Bring along books that will direct you in the Spiritual Disciplines like: *Spiritual Disciplines of a C.H.R.I.S.T.I.A.N.* by Gil Stieglitz; *Celebration of Discipline* by Richard Foster; *The Life You Always Wanted* by Ortmeyer. This should be a time away from your normal life. Don't have a phone, don't watch TV, don't go to a meeting or party... focus on the Lord.

chapter twenty-six

BE ON YOUR GUARD AGAINST TEMPTATION'S HELPERS

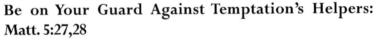

Be on Your Guard Against Temptation's Helpers: Matt. 5:27,28

Jesus is very clear when it comes to dealing with those things that assist lust in winning. **"If your right eye makes you stumble, tear it out and throw it from you; for it is better for you to lose one of the parts of your body, than for your whole body to be thrown into hell. "If your right hand makes you stumble, cut it off and throw it from you; for it is better for you to lose one of the parts of your body, than for your whole body to go into hell."** Notice what Jesus is saying, when something helps you sin then you should be ruthless against it. It seems clear that Jesus does not want us to be gouging out our eyes and cutting off our hands, there are no examples that He ever asked the disciples to do this or moved in this direction Himself. But He does want us to be consistently vigilant about anything that would help lust win. No matter how expensive, precious or irreplaceable, He wants us to remove the offending item from our life.

Sexual temptation has many assistants that help it become more seductive and overwhelming. Often raw lust is able to be overcome somewhat easily, but it is the assistants that allow destructive desires to glide into our lives with greater ease. Let me give you a few examples: If you were at work and a pornographic e-mail were to appear on your screen it would be easy to delete it, especially if your screen faces where lots of people can see it. But if you were watching T.V., late at night, while on a business trip in a distant city and an advertisement for an adult TV program comes on, it is harder to resist going over that and checking it out. The lateness of the night, the distant city and the sensual advertisement assist lust in its battle against you. Another more extreme example of the work of temptation's assistants would be, if a naked woman approaches you in a public place it is easy to resist. But if you know this woman from the office and she approaches you late at night, after a few drinks together, naked except for the trench coat covering her, in hotel room, in a distance city, it may be much tougher to resist.

There are two general kinds of assistants to lust: Sensual assistants and neutral assistants. In the above case the woman and her nakedness are sensuous agents of destructive desire, but it is also the anonymity, the office relationship, the alcohol and the distant city that helps lust and makes it much tougher to resist. We must be alert for both kinds of agents of destructive desires. They do their work differently. One stands out as sensuous and seductive, seeking to entice you into lustful activities. The other agents of lust appear benign and harmless. But both help build a climate where giving in to destructive desires seems like the thing to do.

Set Up Protection Against Temptation's Helpers

You must be prepared for and aware of these aids that strengthen and energize lust. One group of assistants to temptation is sensual assistants: Sensual Music, Sensual Magazines, Sensual Movies, Sensual Stories, Sensual Books, Sensual Friendships, Known Adulteress, Sensual Environments, and Sensual Entertainments. Each of these increases the possibility that you will give in to lust. The goal of these assistants to lust is to create the internal and external environment around you that make it seem that sexual sin is normal, needed, inevitable and wanted. These helpers will focus on the gain of lust rather than the consequences of lust. If one stays in the presence of these assistants they will wear you down until you try their brand of excitement and fun. If you allow them to continually surround you through the music your listen to, the movies you watch, the books and magazines you read, they will fill your head with the wonder of free sex. You have to break away from these helpers. You have to lower and eliminate their influence on your life. This is not always easy.

Resisting the work of these assistants usually means getting rid of magazines, books and even sections of your music collections that emphasize the sexual, or stir up sexual desires in you. It may mean no longer hanging out with certain friends or going to certain types of movies that you have been accustomed to going to. It will mean that you need to substitute righteous alternatives for the ones that use to stir you up in the wrong directions: different magazines, different books, different movies, different friends, different entertainments. It may seem at first that life is boring without all of this "environment" around you. But there are all kinds of righteous alternatives to the wrong type of songs, activities, books, magazines and friends. It only seems like there is nothing because you have not explored all that is out there.

The second group of assistants to lust are much more neutral but maybe even more strategic in their assistance to temptation. These would be: Anonymity, Convenience, Night, Laziness, Arrogance, Discouragement, Alcohol. These helpers cover lust so that it more easily enters your life, and so that you more easily give in. Watch for these helpers and beware of what they are bringing with them. In each of these areas one needs to build safeguards to keep these specific helpers from bringing lust into your life. It is much like a person who offers to carry a bomb for a terrorist organization. It is the bomb that does the damage, but it is the friend that gets it past the usual defenses.

Spiritual Workout

FITNESS

The following are some of the first type of assistants to temptation that will try to break down your resistance to selfishness in the sexual arena. The goal of this examination is to create a positive environment around you so that you can pursue real love and righteousness without being pulled back into selfishness.

Sensual Music: There are all kinds of music that is about the relationships of life. There is a lot of music that sings about illicit sexual relations, trying make it seem like the thing to do. It seeks to spin your mind around the lyrics or the melody so that its message of immoral sexual activity is okay, even good and right. If a type of music stirs up within you desires that you cannot righteously fulfill, then you should take a serious look at removing that from you life.

Some music has such a strong association to particular activities and particular people that hearing it brings back sensual memories and stirs up wrong desires. If this happens, then that music should not be played. At L'abri in Switzerland, a Christian retreat center, Dr. Francis Schaeffer would not allow certain types of music to be played because it would stir up sensual and sinful desires in some of the guests.

Sensual Magazines: There are all kinds of magazines of a sensual nature: from the obvious pornographic to the only sensual in the advertisements. The main question is whether these magazines create a sensual environment around you where it is easier to think, speak and act in a sensual manner. While all pornographic magazines need to be removed from your life, it is important to evaluate which other magazines may also need to be eliminated. Certain sports magazines are needlessly provocative.

Sensual Movies: Our culture is full of movies. Many of these movies are pornographic, some are sensual and others have gratuitous sexual scenes. Many of these movies contribute to the development of a sensual environment and sensual thought process being developed in a person's mind. These movies and scenes become the prescribed behavior for those watching, in some cases. Many people feel a need to watch, repeat and even own movies that have high levels of sensual content. Some men even describe movies by the dominant sex scene in that movie. Some men rent and/or own a movie so that they can watch and rewatch the sensual scene in that movie.

If you are to win the war against lust you must get rid of these sensual and pornographic movies that keep injecting your soul with the wrong goal. It is not until you remove the easy access to sensual conduct and sensual ideas that you will actually create a safe space in your life for clean thoughts and pure actions.

Sensual Stories: There are an endless number of sensual stories and jokes that are often told to keep the sexual and sensual atmosphere thick at work, at parties, at group functions.

Sensual Television: There are an increasing amount of programs on television that are specifically designed to be sensual and provocative. If watching a particular program gets you all sexually wound up then you need to eliminate that program even if other people you know seem to be able to handle it. If you allow your mind to dwell on sensual scenarios by watching television that depicts them you will not win in your battle with destructive desires. If particular shows constantly show scantily clad women then stop watching that show. Too often men do not have the courage to challenge the prevailing wisdom that it is okay to watch anything they want. It may not be illegal but it may be really foolish, robbing you of the joy of real intimacy.

Sensual Books: There are all kinds of books that are designed to stir up sexual passion and tension. These books need to be removed from your life. They act as assistants to the work of lust in your life. They may be fiction, non fiction, manuals, or self-help, but it does not matter if they cause you to be stirred up sensually. Many people try to justify keeping material because it is expensive or classic or no one else is bothered, or it has so much other good material. All of these are excuses to keep a dangerous assistant working in your life. Have the courage to cut it out of your life as Jesus says. "If your right eye causes you to stumble cut it off and throw it from you."

Sensual Friendships: There are two kinds of sensual friendships: First, there are those who stir up sensual desires in you personally because of their desirability. If a particular person stirs up lustful desires within you, then you have an obligation to move away from them and lower the amount of contact with that person. No reason needs to be given, but you must create actual physical and emotional distance between you and that person. Do not try to understand why you are attracted to that person. Do not try to see if you will get over your attraction, just back away from contact and connection with that person. Are there any of these sensual friendships that you need to move away from? Second, there are those whose whole life revolves around sex. These kinds of people whether they are personally desirable or not, spike the air with a sensual tone and orientation. If these people are allowed to remain connected to you without repentance, then they will supercharge the atmosphere with sensuality. Do you know any people like this? How can you move away from consistent contact with these people?

Known Adulteress: If you become aware of a person of the opposite sex who has been involved in adultery and they are becoming flirtatious with you, this is a dangerous relationship. They have already breached the commitment to marital faithfulness. This is especially true when that person is interested in moving their friendship with you to a new level of depth and interaction. Their previous time of infidelity acts as an assistant to mental fantasy and provides an easier bridge to go there again. Do you have any of these relationships? Back out of these kinds of relationships.

Sensual Environments: There are all types of sensually charged situations that increase the likelyhood of giving in to lust. These might include the teen party, the school dance or prom, the late-night hangout with friends far from parents, the hotel bar in a distant city, the restaurant with the sensually attired waitresses, the bachelor party, the bookstore, the movie theater, etc. If a particular activity or environment stirs up in you feelings of desire that you cannot righteously fulfill, then you need to realize that you are being assisted by the environment to lose the battle with lust. You must be willing to eliminate that particular activity or environment to stay pure.

Spiritual Workout

(FITNESS)

The following are some of the most obvious helpers of lust, and some suggestions on what types of safeguards are needed against these friends of a deadly enemy.

Anonymity

When you are not known in a town there is a feeling that you can get away with sin and no one will know. This is especially true when people travel to new cities. No one knows me here, and no one will know what I do.

Safeguards: Bring lots of pictures or reminders of your spouse and family. Set a schedule that your spouse can keep you accountable to. Give your spouse the opportunity to call at any time, but especially those times when lust is most tempting, such as right after dinner and after 10 p.m.

Convenience

One of the tricks of the devil is to make it easy and convenient to sin. This is why there is such a push to tie pornography to free speech. The more convenient it is to sin the more lust and sin will take place. We are by nature lazy creatures who will move to the path of least resistance. So realize that hotels, employers, prostitutes, phone companies, magazines, concierges may make it very easy to give in to lust. These wheelchairs to lust must be avoided. You want to make it very difficult to give in to lust. When something offers to be a convenience to sin, you want to turn it down, get away from it, and bring it into the light.

Safeguards: Have the hotel turn off access to adult channels to your room before you get to the room. Add extra security and filters to your computer which require a password that only your spouse or employer has access to sexually explicit sites. Do not check the mail at work or at your apartment if pornographic magazines will be available to you. Do not go to a newsstand that has pornographic materials available. Refuse to go to company outings or extracurricular outings that involve strip clubs or lascivious behavior. If your employer consistently requires you to entertain or be involved with clients in the context of sensual or lascivious behavior, change jobs, even if it means a cut in pay.

Night Time

It is dark and it seems like no one can see you. It is amazing how much we psychologically believe that the night hides. And the later it gets the more hidden we are tempted to believe our actions have become. This is not true of course but it feels like that to us.

Safeguards: Set up a curfew like 10 p.m. that you will not be out or on the internet or entertaining clients. Turn off the TV or computer late at night so that those temptations are not present.

Laziness

It is hard work to prepare for a battle against lust. It is especially hard when sometimes we secretly want lust to win (at least a little). So we get lazy. We put off the preparations that are necessary to defeat lust. We don't erect strong enough barriers because we are doing okay with this level of protection. We don't always have someone else present when we are seeing a member of the opposite sex at work. We don't increase the level of our internet filter to block the most pornography on our computer. We don't keep a professional distance from those who are attractive or attracted to us. We speak with another about lust as though it was our true feelings. We refuse to enforce the policy regarding adult magazines at work, or relationships at work, or sexual jokes or innuendos. We overlook the posters, t-shirts, pictures, etc., that are very sensual and inappropriate because it is just too much work to be on people all the time.

Safeguards: Work with your spouse to set and keep your boundaries vigilant. Realize that you are at war with lust and if it wins it will eventually destroy all that you have and hold dear. It is not a win to let lust win… it is a loss and relationships and trust will be gone. Keep vigilant. If you think of a way to safeguard yourself, your company, and your family from lust write it down and have a discussion with the appropriate person about implementing this strategy. No one ever thought that everyone who boarded a plane would need to be scanned and searched until a few planes were blown up. Don't allow yourself to become lazy against an enemy that wants to devour you and all that you have built.

Arrogance

One of the consistent characteristics of all those who give in to lust is arrogance. They don't think they will be caught. They think that the normal sexual rules don't apply to them. They think they deserve more sexual attention and favors. They think that they are better than the average person. They believe that they are more important than the average person who must confine his sexual desires to one partner for life. They believe that somehow their abilities or position or wealth has earned them the right to play fast and loose with the normal moral boundaries. The Bible says, "Take heed lest where you think you stand you fall." This is the inner feelings that you are doing well, that you really have made something of yourself. It is inner sense of accomplishment that in and of itself is not bad, but pride piggybacks on this feeling to suggest that normal rules don't apply to you.

Safeguards: Follow the rules. Find your joy inside the God-given boundaries. Be careful not to surround yourself with people who will allow you to have an inflated view of yourself. Make sure that at least once a month you are serving the poor, afflicted, oppressed, down trodden... those who clearly are at a different place than God has allowed you to be. Take time to contemplate your role in terms of all the roles, positions, jobs and relationships in the world at that moment. This means to realize that you have a role to play, but you are just one of many in the world, even if you're President or Prime minister. It is a role and there are lots of other roles. In order for our world to function there are lots of different roles and people doing crucial things or we would cease to function as an economy or culture. There are farmers, planners, water treatment people, police, government officials, educators, truck drivers, sewage treatment people, social workers, pastors, media, entertainers, writers, businessmen, repair people, maintenance people, and sales people who are all required to make a civilization and community function. You are just one of them, even if you are king.

Discouragement

One of the times that lust always attacks is when you are discouraged. You have just went through a difficult time and lust is there to suggest that it can ease your pain by offering you an illicit high. Be very careful when you are discouraged or depressed. Lust will offer you a false way out. Discouragement often becomes a Trojan horse for lust. Rather than face the truth of your loss or the pain of the discouragement, it is always tempting to just cover over discouragement, loss and pain with the medication of lust. Do not do this. Face your pain, deal with the wound or loss. It is not easy but it is essential.

Safeguards: When you're discouraged let some people close to you know. Also let them know before you are discouraged about the connection between discouragement and lust. A man who loses his job is more open to the illicit comfort of the wrong woman. Find a friend who you can fully explore the discouragement with. If there is no friend who is willing to plumb the depths of the depression with you, then find a counselor who will work it through with you. Don't just let discouragement just hang over your life like a blanket without seeking to understand its causes, cures and lessons.

Alcohol and Drugs

Another helper to lust is alcohol and drugs. These lower one's resistance and therefore encourage sexual recklessness. Wherever there is sexual license there is always drugs and alcohol. If you don't give into drunkenness and the artificial highs of drugs you will be able to resist lust's suggestions. People who give in to drinking and the synthetic highs of drugs often push the boundaries of sexual behavior way past what they would normally do, and then that sets up relationships and patterns that are even more difficult to break. Then on top of that, they need more alcohol and drugs to mask the guilt, pain and shame of what they did when they were under their influence initially. It becomes a vicious cycle. Don't go down that road.

Safeguards: If you have not entered into the party scene then don't... just avoid the first drink, the first drag and the first pill, and your battle with lust will be much easier. If you have been involved in drinking and drugs then stop right now. Each day do not drink or take drugs that day. If you have given in to the place of an addiction to these powerful medications, then join a Christian support group where you can be honest and get the level of accountability you need. Remember that there is forgiveness at the foot of the Cross. Realize also that your battle with selfishness is daily and ongoing but will result in new levels of freedom, privilege and opportunity as you win each day. You do not know how God will use you in a few weeks, a few months, a few years, if you do not give in today. Resistance is hard, but it is worth it and we have His energy to assist.

chapter twenty-seven

You Cannot Do Two Things at the Same Time

You cannot do two things at the same time: Gal. 5:16

One of the exciting things about being a Christian is that the Holy Spirit lives within us into and He will guide us into what to do instead of giving into sexual temptation. Scripture states (Gal. 5:16-18) that when fleshly temptation speaks in your heart, that those who are Christian will also have the prompting of the Holy Spirit directing the specific righteous behavior that would be appropriate at the time to defeat the fleshly temptation. If you quickly move to walk by the Spirit then you cannot be doing the prompting of fleshly temptation. Gal. 5:16, 17 says, **"But I say, walk by the Spirit, and you will not carry out the desire of the flesh. For the flesh sets its desire against the Spirit, and the Spirit against the flesh; for these are in opposition to one another, so that you may not do the things that you please."** If the Spirit of God is talking, then the flesh is also trying to tempt or prompt us to do something pleasurable that would harm us or those around us. This means that you have a choice to make regarding whose directions you will take. Will you take the prompting of sin or will you take the prompting of the Holy Spirit. You have a choice but there is really not a third alternative when temptation is trying to seduce you. You must choose to follow one or the other.

Years ago when I was a single man, a rather flirtatious married woman came to the church I was attending. She tried to spend time around various single men in the church, including myself. Her behavior seemed overly flirtatious and so I kept my distance. One time I remember she was insistent that I meet with her and talk about various problems in the church. I had a strong sense from the Holy Spirit that I should not meet with her. So I refused to meet with her and instead scheduled something to do out of town. After this incident, she no longer acted warmly toward me, nor wanted to meet with me. A short time later I became aware that she had started an affair with one of the other single men in the church. It of course ended badly with shame and difficulty on all involved. I realized that God the Holy Spirit had prompted me to be somewhere else other than near this woman. By God's grace and the guidance of the Holy Spirit I was not in a position to fall victim to her seductions. I was somewhere else. And in many cases this is the best defense against sexual temptation. God wants you in a different place, doing a different thing when temptation that is too strong for you comes your way. He will guide you if you listen for the still small voice of His Spirit.

Many Christians are not aware of the oppositional nature of the Holy Spirit and temptation from within. If one is talking then the other is also prompting. It is important to train yourself to listen carefully for the prompting of the Holy Spirit while temptation is pressing on you. Ask God the Holy Spirit to make it clear what He wants you to do. He will make it clear. At the time of the most intense pressure from temptation to give in to lust and selfishness, God the Holy Spirit, if you ask, will prompt you to do a chore, or call a friend, or exercise, or get up and do something else, or write a note, or do homework, etc. It is always doing something else and not just a prompt to not give in to the temptation. You must do something else rather than what the temptation wants you to do. God the Holy Spirit will make it clear what it is that you should do. Sometimes you may think of a person or chore or action that you had not been thinking about. Sometimes the Lord will give you an image of what you should be doing. Other times you will just think of something you should do yourself with the actions of the Holy Spirit much more hidden.

Now it is also true from this verse that when the Holy Spirit is going to prompt you to do something righteous, then the flesh is going to prompt you with a temptation to lust or anger or laziness or some other deed of the flesh. It is all designed so that you must make a choice which master you are going to listen to that day.

Spiritual Workout

We have to train ourselves to listen hard for the prompting of the Spirit of Christ when we feel the pull of temptation.

- What did the Spirit of Christ prompt you to do the last time you felt the pull of lust?

- Which did you choose to do? What lust wanted, or what the Spirit wanted?

- What are the kinds of things that the Spirit of Christ usually prompts people to do when they feel the pull of temptation?

When you face temptation this week listen hard for the Spirit of Christ and obey. Write down here what pressure you faced and what the Holy Spirit prompted.

chapter twenty-eight

GET PHYSICAL DISTANCE BETWEEN YOU AND THE LUSTFUL OBJECT

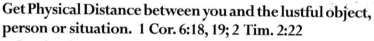

Get Physical Distance between you and the lustful object, person or situation. 1 Cor. 6:18, 19; 2 Tim. 2:22

Lust has the power to tempt only over a certain distance. It is like the remote locking mechanism for cars. They only send their signal so far. Temptation sends out its signal to our eyes, our ears and our touch. If we are within range we will feel this pull. We do not have to give in, but we can increase the likelihood that we will resist by getting distance between us and the temptation. Temptation loses its effectiveness over distance. Therefore Scripture screams at us to get away from lustful things. 1 Cor. 6:18 says, **"Flee immorality. Every *other* sin that a man commits is outside the body, but the immoral man sins against his own body."** 2 Tim. 2:22 says, **"Now flee from youthful lusts and pursue righteousness, faith, love and peace, with those who call on the Lord from a pure heart.** While there may be lustful things all over the city that you live in, if you do not see them or interact with them they have no power over you. Therefore be prepared to just move away from things that are excessively tempting. I remember working with one young man who just walked away from a young lady who was making suggestive comments. Many times we are more afraid of being embarrassed or offending other people rather than being zealous of the glory of God. Walk away just as Joseph did from Potiphar's wife. He was falsely accused and probably thought foolish by the other servants, but He pleased God and eventually his righteousness allowed God to install him as ruler under the Pharaoh. What would have happened if he had not run away from his master's wife? He would have eventually been discovered when Potiphar's wife grew tired of him and then he would have been killed.

Are you prepared to leave a party, walk away from a conversation, walk out of a room, run away from a sensual situation rather than to let lust win? Think through the scenarios that you might face or have faced at work, at a party, with your friends. Picture yourself walking or running away and in that way winning against temptation. Being embarrassed is better than offending God. Have you walked away from a conversation at work that was all about sexual jokes or sexual exploits? Have you refused to enter into a situation where a flirtatious or seductive person was holding sway?

Bill was entertaining Janis at his apartment when the time became supercharged sexually and the only way that Bill could keep from giving in to the moment and Janis's charms was to excuse himself and walk out of the apartment and walk around the block. It worked— neither of them gave into the sexual suggestions that were dancing around in their heads. He was able to explain his conduct to Janis later and she also agreed that it was supercharged situation and his actions broke the power of lust in that situation. Few men have the courage to actually leave their own apartment because lust is winning, but his love for God and his real love for Janis were more important than any personal embarrassment he may have suffered. He won. Do not be afraid to act godly, you win!!!

Spiritual Workout

FITNESS

What are the top 5 ways that lust seeks to tempt you or seduce you?

1.
2.
3.
4.
5.

How are you going to get physical distance from the top 5 elements of lust in your life? Actually write down realistic ways to get physical distance from real temptations and share them with your small group. Your small group may have other suggestions for ways to gain physical distance from certain temptations, or they may not think that your application of this principle is realistic or sufficient. Be open to their suggestions.

1.
2.
3.
4.
5.

chapter twenty-nine

LEARN TO LIVE IN THE FEAR OF GOD

**Learn to live in the fear of God: Luke 12:2; Prov. 2:5; 16:6;
15:16; 8:13; 2 Cor. 5:10; Gal. 6:7; James 1:17**

Throughout Scripture we are told that there is a way of thinking and
living that will make a huge difference in our battle with temptation
and our enjoyment of life. It is called the fear of the Lord. God has said
that the fear of the Lord is the beginning of wisdom. The fear of the
Lord is that way of living that brings joy to the heart of God and does
not activate the natural consequences that God has built into the world
in which we live. Living in the fear of the Lord is like living in a big
spotlight. It is the spotlight of God's pleasure and blessing. Wherever
the spotlight moves, living in the fear of the Lord means staying inside
of its light. When we move outside of the light with our selfish actions
and sinful speech, then the darkness envelopes us and the difficulties
of the darkness wound us. There are five aspects to living in the
fear of the Lord: (1) The desire to please and reverence God with our
actions (Prov. 2:5); (2) The desire to receive the blessings that God
gives to follow His commands (James 1:17; Prov. 15:16); (3) The
realization that there is coming a Judgment Day (2 Cor. 5:10,11); (4)
Embracing the truth that everything we have ever said and done will

be evaluated and seemingly shown to others who may need or want to know (Luke 12:2); (5) God has set up consequences for when we disobey His design for righteous living (Gal. 6:7; Prov. 8:13).

It is an amazing thing to realize that the ultimate reality in the Universe is an all-powerful spirit being we call God. He desires that we understand who He is, and worship Him for who He is and the wonder of creation. We begin to live life the way it was intended when we realize that Almighty God is the center of the Universe. He is watching us all the time and we can please Him with our actions, thoughts, words, attitudes and motives. When we adjust our life in various ways to glorify Him we live in the fear of the Lord. When we gather together with others, who also have come to appreciate the central truth of the Universe, and praise and exalt God the ultimate reality is it produces a new alignment with the purpose of Creation.

God who does not in any way need us has decided to bless those who adjust their lives to His standards and wishes. The Fear of the Lord is a desire to receive as many of those blessings as He wants to bestow upon us. God has promised that if we humble ourselves and admit that we are not the center of the universe and that He is, He will add new measures of grace, power and mercy to our lives (1 Pet. 5:5). The treasuries of God are full of all kinds of spiritual, mental, emotional, even material gifts. The one who lives in the fear of the Lord has determined that it is worth it to diligently seek the Lord (Heb. 11:6).

There is a significant difference between those who realize that there will be a Judgment Day when all of their actions, words, thoughts, attitudes and motives will be evaluated, and those who are blissfully unaware of this coming review. A person who lives in the fear of the Lord embraces the coming Judgment Day and seeks to have more items that will meet with God's approval and commendation. Now the judgment day for believers in the forgiving sacrifice of Jesus Christ will be different than those who are still trying to impress God and earn His favor with their own goodness. Those who have embraced the Lord Jesus as their sacrifice and only reason for access into God's presence will be evaluated at their judgment day for rewardable actions. Do you want God to reward you a lot on Judgment Day, or are you still pretending it is not coming?

When we realize that everything that we ever say, do, think, emote or intend is permanently recorded and waiting for God's scrutiny at the judgment of all mankind, it causes us to realize that every single time that a person can turn away from sin it is a good thing. The fear of the Lord is the truth that God is holy and sees everything and knows everything. The truth that induces the fear of the Lord comes from the verse that says that He will make every hidden thing known and every secret thing will be revealed (Ecc. 12:14; Matt. 12:36; Luke 12:2). There are two ways that that verse could come true. Either Christ will reveal to you in private every single thing that impacted what happened to you on earth, or He will have every person impacted by your decisions looking at the record of your life. Either way you will become aware of all the hidden deals, conniving, secret plans, unknown actions, secrets of others that impacted your life. It may be much like the truth commissions in South Africa a few years back, in which every person was asked to tell what they did and what happened to them during the years of apartied. No one was punished for what they said but it allowed everyone to know what really took place. We must stop pretending that we have a private life that He does not know about or that He doesn't see. He has chosen to forgiven us because of the work of Christ on the cross, but He saw and He knows. He will render to every man according to his deeds. We can in the present choose to put less sin, less that we will regret on the video tape of our lives. Every choice we make to be righteous and avoid sin means that we are fearing the Lord.

The fear of the Lord is also the fact that God has built consequences into every action. We reap what we sow. **"God will not be mocked whatsoever a man sows that shall he also reap."** If we give in to lust and adultery, there will be physical, emotional, mental and spiritual consequences. Some of these consequences are immediate, such as relational breakups and financial losses. Other consequences take days, weeks, even years to unfold. I have included in one of the Spiritual Workouts a list of the various sexually transmitted diseases and their symptoms to remind you and me that God will not be mocked. It is a fearful thing to fall into the hands (consequences) of the Living God.

I remember one man telling me, "I don't want Jesus coming back and have Him find me masturbating and looking at dirty pictures." "I need to stop this." When confronted with the truth of Christ's searching gaze, many people get serious about holiness in their lives. The truth of a Christian Worldview allows people to live in the fear of the Lord. Because many Christians do not understand the truth of Christian doctrine, it is much harder for them to live in harmony with that truth.

Spiritual Workout

Write out a card with the 5 elements of the fear of the Lord on it.
Read and re-read the card every hour on the hour for three days.

5 Aspects of the Fear of the Lord	Verses:
1) The desire to please and reverence God with our actions;	Prov. 2:5 Then you will discern the **fear of the Lord** and discover the knowledge of God.
2) The desire to receive the blessings that God gives to follow His commands;	James 1:17 Every good thing given and every perfect gift is from above, coming down from the Father of lights, with whom there is no variation or shifting shadow. Prov. 15:16 "Better is a little with the **fear of the Lord** than great treasure and turmoil with it."
3) The realization that there is coming a Judgment Day;	2 Cor. 5:10, 11 For we must all appear before the judgment seat of Christ, so that each one may be recompensed for his deeds in the body, according to what he has done, whether good or bad. Therefore, knowing the fear of the Lord, we persuade men, but we are made manifest to God.

4) Embracing the truth that everything we have ever said and done will be evaluated and seemingly shown to others who may need or want to know;	Luke 12:2 "But there is nothing covered up that will not be revealed, and **hidden** that will not be known."
5) God has set up consequences for when we disobey His design for righteous living.	Gal. 6:7 Do not be deceived, God is not mocked; for whatever a man sows, this he will also reap. Prov. 8:13"The **fear of the Lord** is to hate evil; Pride and arrogance and the evil way And the perverted mouth, I hate."

Spiritual Workout

Write down in the next three days three things that you avoided rather than have them on the video tape of your life.

1.
2.
3.
4.
5.

Spiritual Workout

Write down five things that you will do in the next three days that would please the Lord.

1.
2.
3.
4.
5.

Spiritual Workout

Write down five blessings that God has given you because of living inside of the fear of the Lord.

1.

2.

3.

4.

5.

Spiritual Workout

Read through the following list of some of the sexually transmitted diseases that can be contracted by abandoning God's plan for sexual fulfillment and intimacy.

Sexually Transmitted Disease (STD)	Symptoms of Sexually Transmitted Disease (STD)
	"An estimated 300,000 infants die or suffer birth defects every year because of VD infections they get from their mothers. (Consequences of VD for Women and Children, American Social Health Association, 260 Sheridan Ave, Ste.207 Palo Alto, CA 94306) "At least seven cancers have been associated with different STD's, five with human papilloma (anal carcinoma, carcinoma of the cervix, cervical intraepithelial neplasia, penile carcinoma, and vulvar carcinoma), one with Hepatitis B and others HIV infection." (Information requested from the Centers for Disease Control by telephone, Jan, 1990)

Bacterial Vaginosis (BV)	Most women have no symptoms. Women with symptoms may have: vaginal itching; pain when urinating; discharge with a fishy odor. (United States Government web site regarding sexually transmitted diseases and their impact on women. *www.4women.gov/faq/stdsgens*) Bacterial Vaginosis (BV) is the name of a condition in women where the normal balance of bacteria in the vagina is disrupted and replaced by an overgrowth of certain bacteria. It is sometimes accompanied by discharge, odor, pain, itching, or burning. (Center for Disease Control website: *www.cdc.gov/std*)
Chlamydia:	Most women have no symptoms. Women with symptoms may have: abnormal vaginal discharge; burning when urinating; bleeding between menstrual periods. Infections that are not treated, even if there are no symptoms, can lead to: lower abdominal pain; low back pain; nausea; fever; pain during sex; bleeding between periods. (United States Government web site regarding sexually transmitted diseases and their impact on women. *www.4women.gov/faq/stdsgens*) Chlamydia is a common sexually transmitted disease (STD) caused by the bacterium, *Chlamydia trachomatis*, which can damage a woman's reproductive organs. Even though symptoms of chlamydia are usually mild or absent, serious complications that cause irreversible damage, including infertility, can occur "silently" before a woman ever recognizes a problem. Chlamydia also can cause discharge from the penis of an infected man. (Center for Disease Control website: *www.cdc.gov/std*) Women infected with chlamydia are up to five times more likely to become infected with HIV, if exposed. (Center for Disease Control website: *www.cdc.gov/std*)

| Genital Herpes | Some people may have no symptoms. During an "outbreak," the symptoms are clear: small red bumps, blisters, or open sores on the penis, vagina, or on areas close by; vaginal discharge; fever; headache; muscle aches; pain when urinating; itching, burning, or swollen glands in genital area; pain in legs, buttocks, or genital area. (United States Government web site regarding sexually transmitted diseases and their impact on women. *www.4women.gov/faq/stdsgens*)

"Genital herpes is a sexually transmitted disease (STD) caused by the herpes simplex viruses type 1 (HSV-1) and type 2 (HSV-2). When signs do occur, they typically appear as one or more blisters on or around the genitals or rectum. The blisters break, leaving tender ulcers (sores) that may take two to four weeks to heal the first time they occur." (Center for Disease Control website: *www.cdc.gov/std*)

"Women who reported having genital warts were 15 times more likely to develop vulvar cancer as those who never had such warts, and those who repeated episodes of genital warts were 36 times as likely to develop vulvar cancer." (Pampillomavirus Infection Among Factors That May Raise Vulvar Cancer Risk," Family Planning Perspectives, September/October 1991, p.48)

"I have begun telling those patients of mine who seem interested in knowing the cause of their cervical dysplasia, cervical cancer or venereal warts, that they are sexually transmitted disease almost entirely." (Joe S. McIhaney, MD, CMS Journal, Winger, V.XIII, No. 1, p 27) |
| Gonorrhea | Symptoms are often mild, but most women have no symptoms. Even when women have symptoms, they can sometimes be mistaken for a bladder or another vaginal infection. Symptoms are: pain or burning when urinating; yellowish and sometimes bloody |

	vaginal discharge; bleeding between menstrual periods. (United States Government web site regarding sexually transmitted diseases and their impact on women. *www.4women.gov/faq/stdsgens*) **Gonorrhea** is caused by *Neisseria gonorrhoeae*, a bacterium that can grow and multiply easily in the warm, moist areas of the reproductive tract, including the cervix (opening to the womb), uterus (womb), and fallopian tubes (egg canals) in women, and in the urethra (urine canal) in women and men. The bacterium can also grow in the mouth, throat, eyes, and anus. (Center for Disease Control website: *www.cdc.gov/std*) "As many as 1,000,000 women are made sterile by gonorrhea each year in the US, while 6% of women who have had just one gonorrhea infection will end up totally sterile." (Sexually transmitted diseases, In Focus, June 1991. Note. 700 Thirteen Street. NW, Ste. 500, Washington D.C. 02005)
Hepatitis B	Some women have no symptoms. Women with symptoms may have: mild fever; headache and muscle aches; tiredness; loss of appetite; nausea or vomiting; diarrhea; dark-colored urine and pale bowel movements; stomach pain; skin and whites of eyes turning yellow. (United States Government web site regarding sexually transmitted diseases and their impact on women. *www.4women.gov/faq/stdsgens*) **Hepatitis B** is a serious disease caused by a virus that attacks the liver. The virus, which is called hepatitis B virus (HBV), can cause lifelong infection, cirrhosis (scarring) of the liver, liver cancer, liver failure, and death. Symptoms of Hepatitis B are: jaundice, fatigue, abdominal pain, loss of appetite, nausea, vomiting, joint pain. (Center for Disease Control website: *www.cdc.gov/std*)
HIV/AIDS	Attacks the immune system; it opens the body to other infections that it would normally be able to fight

	off; it results in death. It brings on a susceptibility to a number of painful physical and psychological problems, including Karposki sarcoma, pneumonia dementia, tuberculosis, etc. Some women may have no symptoms for 10 years or more. Women with symptoms may have: extreme fatigue; rapid weight loss; frequent low-grade fevers and night sweats; frequent yeast infections (in the mouth); vaginal yeast infections and other STDs; pelvic inflammatory disease (PID); menstrual cycle changes; red, brown, or purplish blotches on or under the skin or inside the mouth, nose, or eyelids. (United States Government web site regarding sexually transmitted diseases and their impact on women. *www.4women.gov/faq/stdsgens*) **HIV/AIDS** Individuals who are infected with STDs are at least two to five times more likely than uninfected individuals to acquire HIV if they are exposed to the virus through sexual contact. In addition, if an HIV-infected individual is also infected with another STD, that person is more likely to transmit HIV through sexual contact than other HIV-infected persons. (Wasserheit, 1992). (Center for Disease Control website: *www.cdc.gov/std*)
Human Papillomavirus (HPV)	Some women have no symptoms. Women with symptoms may have: visible warts in the genital area, including the thighs. Warts can be raised or flat, alone or in groups, small or large, and sometimes they are cauliflower-shaped; lesions on the cervix and in the vagina. (United States Government web site regarding sexually transmitted diseases and their impact on women. *www.4women.gov/faq/stdsgens*)
Pubic Lice	Symptoms: itching; finding lice. (United States Government web site regarding sexually transmitted diseases and their impact on women. *www.4women.gov/faq/stdsgens*)

Syphilis	Symptoms in the first, or primary stage: a single, painless sore appears, usually in the genital areas but may appear in the mouth; if infection is not treated, it moves to the next stage.
	Symptoms in the next, or secondary, stage are: skin rash on the hands and feet that usually does not itch and clears on its own; fever; swollen lymph glands; sore throat; patchy hair loss; headaches; weight loss; muscle aches; tiredness.
	In the latent, or hidden, stage, the symptoms listed above disappear, but the symptoms from the second stage can come back. In the late stage, infection remains in the body and can damage the brain, nerves, eyes, heart, blood vessels, liver, bones, and joints. (United States Government web site regarding sexually transmitted diseases and their impact on women. *www.4women.gov/faq/stdsgens*)
	Syphilis is a sexually transmitted disease (STD) caused by the bacterium *Treponema pallidum.* Syphilis is passed from person to person through direct contact with a syphilis sore. Sores occur mainly on the external genitals, vagina, anus, or in the rectum. Sores also can occur on the lips and in the mouth. Transmission of the organism occurs during vaginal, anal, or oral sex. Pregnant women with the disease can pass it to the babies they are carrying. (Center for Disease Control website: *www.cdc.gov/std*)
Trichomoniasis	Symptoms usually appear 5 to 28 days after exposure and can include: yellow, green, or gray vaginal discharge (often foamy) with a strong odor; discomfort during sex and when urinating; irritation and itching of the genital area; lower abdominal pain in rare cases. (United States Government web site regarding sexually transmitted diseases and their impact on women. *www.4women.gov/faq/stdsgens*)

	Some women have signs or symptoms of infection which include a frothy, yellow-green vaginal discharge with a strong odor. The infection also may cause discomfort during intercourse and urination, as well as irritation and itching of the female genital area. In rare cases, lower abdominal pain can occur. Symptoms usually appear in women within 5 to 28 days of exposure. (Center for Disease Control website: *www.cdc.gov/std*) **Trichomoniasis** is caused by the single-celled protozoan parasite, *Trichomonas vaginalis*. The vagina is the most common site of infection in women, and the urethra (urine canal) is the most common site of infection in men. The parasite is sexually transmitted through penis-to-vagina intercourse or vulva-to-vulva (the genital area outside the vagina) contact with an infected partner. Women can acquire the disease from infected men or women, but men usually contract it only from infected women. (Center for Disease Control website: *www.cdc.gov/std*)
Pelvic Inflammatory Disease (PID)	**(PID)** is a generic term for <u>infection</u> of the female <u>uterus</u>, <u>fallopian tubes</u>, and/or <u>ovaries</u> as it progresses to scar formation with adhesions to nearby tissues and organs. This may lead to tissue <u>necrosis</u> with or without <u>abscess</u> formation. <u>Pus</u> can be released into the peritoneum. 2/3 of patients with <u>laparoscopic</u> evidence of previous PID were not aware they had had PID (Cecil's 5th ed). PID is often associated with <u>sexually transmitted diseases</u>, as it is a common result of such infections. PID is a vague term and can refer to viral, fungal, parasitic, though most often bacterial infections. (*http://en.wikipedia.org/wiki/Pelvic_inflammatory_disease*) PID is the most rapidly increasing cause of infertility in the United States and is the primary reason for the 500% increase in ectoptic pregnancies since 1970. (Dr. Hugh Barber, Female Patient, V14, April, 1989)

Spiritual Workout

Write down 5 things that you have done instead of giving into temptation and destructive desire.

1.

2

3.

4.

5.

chapter thirty

TREAT INTERNET PORNOGRAPHY AS A RADIOACTIVE SUBSTANCE

Treat Internet Pornography as a Radioactive Toxic Substance or a Highly Addictive Drug

There is fascinating new research that gives insight into why Internet pornography is capturing and addicting men to a much higher degree and in greater numbers than ever before. Internet pornography is not the same problem as looking at pictures of naked women in your friend's garage. Internet pornography is a highly addictive drug designed to addict men through the stimulation of multiple chemical, psychological, emotional and sexual triggers. Internet pornography is a new dangerous construct based on hundreds of hours of detailed studies in the structure and interests of male brains. This is a new form of pornography that can addict with the first use. Through stimulation of brain chemicals, emotional responses and software traps, internet pornographers are pushing a much more addictive and destructive product than the airbrushed photos of the past.

- Pornography has become a $57 billion industry worldwide.

- It produces more revenue in the United States than the combined revenues of all professional football, baseball and basketball franchises or the combined revenues of ABC, CBS, and NBC.

- It robs the workplace of the time and talents of employees. 20% of men admit accessing pornography at work. 13% of women do so.

- One in five children ages 10-17 has received a sexual solicitation over the Internet.

- Compiled by Content Watch (*www.contentwatch.com*)

Listen to Mark Kastlemen who compiled the various studies and research articles he has posted on ContentWatch.com and in his powerful book, ***The Drug of the New Millennium—The Science of How Internet Pornography Radically Alters the Human Brain and Body—A Guide for Parents, Spouses, Clergy and Counselors.*** There is so much impacting material that this writer has been forced to take the highlights of this article and strongly urge you to read Dr. Kastlemen's articles and purchase his book.

> "Internet pornographers are some of the most cunning, degenerate marketers and salespeople in the entire world—physical or virtual. They know their craft and have devised laser-focus techniques to capture each of those markets. Based on the structure of the male brain, how do Internet pornographers market to men and teenage boys?"

> **Visual Stimulation at the Highest Possible Level**
> "Knowing that the typical male viewer's primary perception is vision, pornographers have crammed the Internet with every visual stimuli that exists—

photographs, videos, live camera, cartoons, virtual reality, etc."

"Once inside the porn site, the viewer is splattered with a visual overload.... An unending stream of visual stimuli as fast and constantly changing as the male viewer desires—a critical element because without a constantly changing visual display, the male brain quickly grows bored."

Male Viewers Want to See Body Parts Pornographers know full well the male brain's predisposition to narrowly focus on parts rather than the whole—to objectify and compartmentalize everything. Internet porn geared to the male audience is a continuous wave of one specific male body part doing everything imaginable to every conceivable female body part, from head to toe. ...completely devoid of any emotion, romance or tenderness."

Dominance, Aggression, and Violence in Male-Centered Porn "As discussed previously, the more cellular memories (biological and physiological processes) that pornographers can link their porn to throughout the male brain and body, the greater chance they have of addicting their viewers. And the more naturally occurring drugs/hormones (especially testosterone, but also adrenaline, epinephrine, and others) flowing in the male mind-body during viewing, the more narrow will be his focus, the more intense his sexual/mind-body arousal, the more deeply the images will be imprinted in his memory, and the greater his addiction."

"Pornographers achieve this combination of a high number of mind-body links and maximum drug/hormone release by mixing sexual images with male dominance, aggression and violent images intended to shock and stimulate simultaneously."

"These kinds of images link sexual arousal in the male mind-body with emotions of shock, anger, confusion, violence and domination which cause the male mind-body to release enormous amounts of additional testosterone, which further increase male narrowing, loss of reason, feelings of aggression, and sexual drive and arousal."

"Internet porn of this ilk creates a chain reaction in the male mind-body with hundreds of hormonal, chemical, emotional, physiological and biological processes all converging at once!"

"The male viewer is not only addicted to simple sexual arousal, but this arousal is linked to mind-body processes that would never be normally linked to the sexual process. Talk about addiction at a whole new level! This would be like a drug addict shooting up with a dozen different hard-core drugs all at once." (Mark Kastlemen, ContentWatch., 2006 www.contentwatch.com)

The level of sophistication and intentional manipulation now built into Internet pornography means that it is toxic and highly corrosive to the soul. Internet pornography cannot be treated with kid gloves. It is highly addictive and deeply destructive. Men who have successfully beaten other forms of lust are falling prey to this new multiple-pronged attack. Most people believe that this form of pornography is like all other forms of pornography that has come before it. It is not!!! People must be alerted to this new danger. We must build new high level defenses and understand the concentrated poisonous nature of this substance.

Realize that the goal of this new form of pornography is to quickly bring about addiction to viewing this stuff. If they can addict you, they have most likely have created a consistent revenue stream through your "need" to view these images. This material is designed to flood your system with nine or more different pleasure creating chemicals and anchor your interest through sexual climax. This scenario often creates addiction in one session. If they can get a man to masturbate to climax they most likely have you.

Teens, college students, pastors, businessmen, professionals, professors and many others are being ensnared in this radically destructive form of lust. These men have fallen victim to something that they never saw coming and that attacked them with a level of toxicity that was overwhelming. Many men have lost jobs, careers, marriages, scholarships, reputations, and in some cases their freedom, because they did not have enough respect for the incredible danger that is Internet pornography.

DO NOT TREAT THIS LIGHTLY.

IT IS NOT YOUR FATHER'S PORNOGRAPHY.

Spiritual Workout

FITNESS

Since Internet pornography is an active toxin designed to produce addiction quickly, Internet pornography must dealt with, with an unusual level of protocol and security.

Have the computer monitor in a public place or facing a public area.

Install filters and blocking software that will not allow you to visit Internet pornography sites even by mistake.

Install an accountability program to the family (and potentially the work) computer that will e-mail every web site that is visited to trusted accountability partners.

Use a filtered Internet Service Provider that blocks pornography at the server. Examples are Arilion, Mayberry, Content Watch, etc.

This material is designed to steal your soul, and your ability to enjoy your family. It is highly addictive and destructive. Do not assume that you will be immune from its effects. Take action to protect yourself. You must take extra precautions. Submitting to the above level of accountability does not mean that you are weak. It means that you are smart enough to realize the danger of this menace.

Some men tell me that yes they look at pornography on the internet, but they are not addicted to it. This is the classic denial scenario. I usually ask them to prove to themselves that they are not addicted by not viewing pornography in any form for 7 days. Often men are not aware of the addictive need that has been created in their life until they try to go without it. That strong almost irresistible pull that you feel to view the material is your addiction. If you cannot go 7 days without it, then you are addicted and you need help, and you need to get serious about this toxin in your life.

chapter thirty-one

INCREASE EXERCISE AND PERSONAL DISCIPLINE

Increase Exercise and Personal Discipline: 1 Cor. 9:24-27; 1 Tim. 4:7,8; Eph. 5:15,16; Rom. 13:13

The more lazy and undisciplined you are about your life, the harder it will be to resist temptation. Everyone feels better if they are working out, getting proper sleep and keeping busy. Lust is sure to find a easier victory if your life is not tuned up. Single men especially need to exercise and get proper amounts of sleep because these are two of the main ways that they will release sexual energy in a righteous way. Exercise burns up excess energy and channels our remaining energies to productive purposes. Eight-plus hours of sleep per night allows for a rested and restored individual, but it also allows for the appropriate mechanism of night dreams to function so that a man can release his sperm build-up through non-sexual contact. A well-ordered schedule with appropriate levels of work, rest, friends, activities, and the like, significantly helps in the battle with lust.

Listen to what the Scripture admonishes us in regards to exercise and personal discipline. The Apostle Paul talks about his plan to control his body in 1 Cor. 9:24-27, **"Do you not know that those** who run in a race all run, but only one receives the prize? Run in such a way that you may win. Everyone who competes in the games exercises self-control in all things. They then do it to receive a perishable wreath, but we an imperishable. Therefore I run in such a way, as not without aim; I box in such a way, as not beating the air; but I discipline my body and make it my slave, so that, after I have preached to others, I myself will not be disqualified."

Again the Apostle Paul visits the whole area of discipline, exercise and self-control when near the end of his life he writes to his son in the faith Timothy (1 Tim. 4:7, 8) **"But have nothing to do with worldly fables fit only for old women. On the other hand, discipline yourself for the purpose of godliness; for bodily discipline is only of little profit, but godliness is profitable for all things, since it holds promise for the present life and also for the life to come."** This is a remarkable passage because he gives insight into the fact that one must discipline oneself so that the spiritual disciplines can be practiced. He agrees that exercise is of some value, while he seeks to emphasize how much greater value are the spiritual disciplines of godliness.

Rom. 13:13 also makes it clear that we must be able to control our schedules, bodies, minds and activities so that we do not give in to laziness and temptation. **"Let us behave properly as in the day, not in carousing and drunkenness, not in sexual promiscuity and sensuality, not in strife and jealousy."** A healthy amount of exercise, rest, planning, sleep and personal care will allow us to be more prepared to fight off the attacks of sexual temptation.

Spiritual Workout:
Exercise and
Personal Discipline

Exercise:

The following exercises should be completed each week. If you have any medical conditions please consult your doctor before starting any exercise program.

Do a hundred sit-ups or "crunches" at least three days this week.

Run or walk at least 3 miles (3 days this week).

Alternative: Swim 25 laps of an Olympic size pool (3 days this week).

Do 25 straight leg push-ups (three days this week).

Alternative: Do 3 sets of 10 bicep curls with weights (3 days this week).

Do 3 sets of 10 bench-press (3 days this week).

Do 3 sets of 10 lat pull downs (3 days this week).

Do 3 sets of shoulder raises (3 days this week).

Sleep:

Go to bed no later than 10 or 11 p.m. every night this week.

Get up at 6 or 7 a.m. every day this week.

Establish a normal bedtime and a normal getting up time.

Turn off the television and the computer at bedtime.

Schedule:

Divide your schedule into three major parts: Morning, Afternoon, Evening.

Put at least one significant relational building activity in each part of your day.

Remember work is a relationship that needs to be developed.

Which part of your day are you most likely to face temptation to lust?

What do you need to do to prepare that part of your day to resist temptation?

chapter thirty-two

GET MARRIED

God's Remedy to Sexual Need: Get Married: 1 Cor. 7:8, 9

Paul was a strong Christian in his late 20's. He was having a real problem with lust. He said nothing was working anymore. We had talked a few years before and I had assigned him a number of the exercises in this book. They worked great, but now he made an appointment to ask me what to do since he was so regularly battling with lust and not having near the level of victory that he had previously. We talked about a few more ways to win against the battle with lust. But I also said if Biblical assignments do not work against lust, then it is time to think about getting married and meet the legitimate sexual need within God's prescribed boundaries.

I showed him what the Scripture says in 1 Cor. 7:8, 9 **"But I say to the unmarried and to widows that it is good for them if they remain even as I. But if they do not have self-control, let them marry; for it is better to marry than to burn *with passion*."**

He said that he was not dating anyone. I told him to continue to do everything he could to resist lust, but also to keep his eyes open for a woman whom God might send. Sure enough not a month later he ran into an old friend from high school who was not married. They hit it off and in a very short period of time made plans to marry. God provided a way of escape for this man through marriage. Sometimes men are afraid of commitment to marriage which causes them to have a greater battle with lust. If God has called you to singleness, then His methods of controlling sexual impulse will work. If they no longer work for you, then you should look at getting married.

I have watched God work in this way a number of times. A young man is not sure whether he should get married, so I ask him how his battle with temptation is going. If he is able to apply Biblical projects to his life to fight lust and this brings about victory, then great, continue to serve the Lord as a single person. You will never be as free to serve the Lord as when you are single. If however the young man applies Biblical projects to his life and he cannot achieve a high level of victory in his battle with lust, then it is probably time to think about being married.

There is a new phenomena among younger people that is growing in a number of larger cities to wait until their 30's or 40's to get married. This can be a wonderful way to serve the Lord with more focus and energy before having the responsibilities of a spouse and family. This, however, can put extra strain on a young person in their battle with destructive desires. This is what the Apostle Paul was recommending for those who are single (1 Cor. 7:25-35). But if this extra singleness is used for selfish purposes, then it often increases the temptation to sin. God has said if you cannot control your impulse for sexual intimacy, then you need to get married to quiet the physiological and relational side of lust's power.

The Biblical advice in this chapter should not be construed as encouragement to rush into a marriage with just anyone. The decision to get married should not be made quickly. But neither should it be needlessly avoided. I have known men and women who are trying to stay single for monetary, educational, parental, cultural, selfish, personal, and emotional reasons, when it is clear that they should bring one of their relationships in their life to a marital conclusion.

I can remember one man who kept waiting for Miss Perfect to come along. He was struggling and losing in his battle with temptation. While he kept waiting, he had an off-and-on girlfriend who was perfect for him. He had this idea that his wife should be his ideal everything. Finally a wise pastor pulled this young man aside and asked him why he had not married this young lady. The Pastor pointed out the young lady's many great points, and told the young man to grow up and get over his adolescent fantasy about the perfect woman. The young man in effect had the scales pulled from his eyes and married this wonderful "imperfect" Christian woman. They have a wonderful marriage.

1 Cor. 7:36-38

But if anyone feels he ought to marry because he has trouble controlling his passions, it is all right; it is not a sin; let him marry. But if a man has the willpower not to marry and decides that he doesn't need to and won't, he has made a wise decision. So the person who marries does well, and the person who doesn't marry does even better

The Living Bible

Spiritual Workout:

If you were to be really honest right now: Are you winning in your battle with lust? Yes / No

Make a list of the Spiritual Exercises that you have used in your battle with sexual temptation. Put an X by the ones that have worked in the past. Put a Z by the ones that are currently working.

1.
2.
3.
4.
5.
6.
7.
8.
9.
10.

If God wanted you to get married who are the potential candidates that He might be sending you?

1.
2.
3.
4.
5.

Pray a prayer to ask for God's strength or a mate:
Dear Heavenly Father:

I am doing all I can to serve You and win the battle against sexual temptation. It seems that I can no longer win in the war without having a mate. I would ask You to send me a mate that perfectly fits Your plans for my life, or send me a new level of energy and wisdom to really love people rather than give in to lust.

In the name of the Lord Jesus Christ,
Amen.

If you have a difficult time establishing a healthy relationship with a member of the opposite sex, then ask some people you trust (usually not peers) to coach you in how to get a good relationship started and/or maintained. This may include clothing, hygiene, habits, listening skills, social skills, etc.

chapter thirty-three

REGULAR SEXUAL ENCOUNTERS WITH YOUR SPOUSE

Regular Sexual Encounters With Your Spouse 1 Cor. 7:2-4

One of the surest ways to increase lust in a married man is to have him endure infrequent or long time periods between sexual relations with his wife. On the other hand consistent sexual connection with one's spouse lowers the internal interest in sexual activity. It is important to realize that regular sexual activity with one's spouse does not eliminate lust, it just lowers the physiological pressure that builds towards sexual release. Male physiology tells us that a man produces millions of sperm per day. When these build up to approximately 400 million to 500 million, they need to be released. That biological pressure to release sperm creates a great interest in sexual contact. In some men this build-up occurs every other day. In some men that build-up takes place over a week or longer. But each man has a cycle of sperm production and release.

The Apostle Paul addresses this issue in Scripture: **"But because of immoralities, each man is to have his own wife, and each woman is to have her own husband. The husband must fulfill his duty to his wife, and likewise also the wife to her husband. The wife** does not have authority over her own body, but the husband *does;* and likewise also the husband does not have authority over his own body, but the wife *does.* Stop depriving one another, except by agreement for a time, so that you may devote yourselves to prayer, and come together again so that Satan will not tempt you because of your lack of self-control" (1 Cor. 7:2-5). Notice that God through the Apostle says that husband and wife must meet each other's needs. God has designed regular sexual contact in marriage as a way of combating immorality. This passage does not mean that a husband can force his wife to have sexual relations with him as often as he wants in exactly the way he wants. It does mean that a husband and wife need to work out how their spouse can meet their sexual and romantic needs in various ways.

Partners in marriage need to understand each other's sexual cycles. A woman's cycle usually reaches a peak of interest physiologically for a short period once a month. A man's sexual cycle reaches its peak (for men under 50) every 2 to 7 days. These different sexual timeclocks create an opportunity for great disagreement and discussion. A typical wife needs to understand that her husband is physiologically going to be interested in sexual contact 4 to 16 times more than she will be. Her understanding and willingness to meet this need in her husband will go a long way in helping him win in his battle against lust. They need to work out various ways to meet this need within the context of their schedules. Remember a man is much more tempted to view pornography or contemplate adultery if he has no consistent sexual release in his marriage.

It is absolutely crucial that couples have an open and honest discussion about the frequency and intensity of sex with their marriage. A man cannot expect his wife to be passionate and engaged all the time, as she does not have the same need for physical intimacy as her husband. Couples that have good marriages have usually come to an understanding about sex that is mutually beneficial. They understand that marital sex involves multiple levels, types and times of sexual intimacy. Many couples have recognized at least three different levels of intensity for sexual activity within the rhythm of a marriage. I often suggest to couples that they establish some basic plan for sexual encounters like, once a month a high intensity romantic sexual engagement that may correspond to her peak interest. This might involve a romantic weekend away, or a time when the kids are gone, or a long date. A second level of more regular sexual encounter is also needed. This weekly "normal" sexual connection keeps them connected. This may involve a date and a much shorter time of physical intimacy. It may be mutually stimulating or just satisfying for the husband. Finally, I recommend that the couple have agreed on quickies that will meet the husband's need for release, but do not necessarily involve his wife's being romantically interested. Each of these levels of sexual encounters has a half a dozen or more scenarios that could accomplish these purposes. A couple could use the questions at the end of this chapter to begin the discussion.

It is important that a husband understand that his wife has needs that outrank her need for sexual relations. Her need for honor and conversation are often higher priorities than her need for sexual relations. In fact, her interest in meeting his need for intimacy can be greatly strengthened if he works hard at meeting her high priority needs. (For further discussions read, *Becoming a Godly Husband*, by Gil Stieglitz.)

Spiritual Workouts:

Meeting a Man's Regular Need for Sexual Release

Figure out how often the husband needs sexual release.

It is important to understand how regularly a married couple need sexual release. These numbers will be different for men than for women. With advance in age there is usually a decrease in sexual need and responsiveness. Sexual need and responsiveness is also affected by certain physical, emotional and/or medical conditions. Usually a man's interest is much greater than a woman's, but occasionally this situation is reversed.

What is the man's need for sexual response/release?

2 days, 3 days, 4 days, 5 days, 6 days, 7 days, 8 days, 9 days, 10 days, 11 days, 12 days, 13 days, 14 days, or more?

What is the woman's need for sexual response/release?

2 days, 3 days, 4 days, 5 days, 6 days, 7 days, 8 days, 9 days, 10 days, 11 days, 12 days, 13 days, 14 days, or more?

Make provisions to regularly meet a man's more frequent need for sexual release.

A husband and wife need to have clear expressions and ways to express each others need for sexual release. Frank and open discussions about ways of providing sexual release and connection is radically important.

Which positions are acceptable to you and your spouse?

1.

2.

3.

4.

5.

What are acceptable methods for sexual interaction and release?

> Quick:
>
> Normal:
>
> Extensive:

What are acceptable levels of involvement for both parties?

Align sexual expectations:

It is important for couples to openly discuss their sexual expectations. The following is a formal, some what wooden way of opening the discussion but it can bring out the topic for honest interaction. Both parties should feel free to put their expectations in the statement below. There will need to be grace and flexibility as the discussion grows.

I,_____ would like to have sexual connection with you, my spouse, every _____ number of days. These may be Quick, Normal, or Extensive in their level of involvement.

While this may seem rather blunt, these kinds of discussions can clear up a source of great frustration in marriages. When everybody is on the same page with their expectations in the sexual arena it can have wonderful results. When handled well, clear sexual guidelines in marriage significantly reduce the fleshly pressure of lust.

I,_____(name)_____ need ____(number)____ different ways to meet your sexual needs.

chapter thirty-four

NO OPPOSITE SEX FRIENDSHIPS ONCE YOU'RE MARRIED

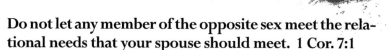

Do not let any member of the opposite sex meet the relational needs that your spouse should meet. 1 Cor. 7:1

One of the consistent facts of adultery is that one of the partners began to allow another person to meet the deep relational needs in their lives which are designed to be met by one's spouse. If you refuse to allow another person to meet your deepest relational needs, then you will not be tempted to move into adultery. It would be better to be thought of as a little cold rather than to encourage an unprofessional relationship with a member of the opposite sex. Deep friendships with members of the opposite sex almost always prompt sexual thoughts and are therefore unwise.

What are men and women's marital relational needs?

I have written extensively about these needs in my books *"Becoming a Godly Husband"* and *"Becoming a Godly Wife,"* but let me give you an overview of these needs here. A woman has a need for her number one man to give her Honor every day and treat her as the most important person, possession or priority in his life (next to God). She has a need for him to Understand her. This would include her way of thinking, her preferences, her temperament, her weaknesses, her sensitivities, her fears, etc. She has a deep need that her husband would build Security in their marriage through financial stability, emotional stability, verbal encouragement and physical stability. She has a need for her husband to Build Unity into their relationship through always being on the same team with her, and building shared experiences with her. She has a need for him to build a system of agreement so that differences of opinion can be resolved, and difficult decisions can be made wisely. She has a need for him to nurture her spiritually with leadership, mentally with conversation, emotionally with romance, physically with tender touch. She also has a need for him to Defend her against various threats and fears that keep her from being all she can be for the glory of God.

A man has a need for his wife to meet the following deep relational needs: He has a need for her to respect and admire him by focusing on his strengths and intent. He has a need for her to Adapt to his world, his temperament, his weaknesses, his leadership, his career, etc. He has a need for her to supply high levels of Domestic Leadership—ordering and creating a stable home and family environment. He has a need for his wife to engage him in sexual Intimacy in a positive and regular manner. He has a need for his wife to become his Companion and share his joy in various activities and dreams. He has a need for his wife to continue developing an Attractive Soul and Body. He finally has a need for his wife to Listen to him so that he can share the secrets of his heart with her.

Spiritual Workout

Meet your spouse's relational needs.

Look at the list of relational needs that are listed below and mentioned above and commit to doing more on one of the needs of your spouse to evidence your love for them.

Honor	Respect
Understanding	Adapt
Security	Domestic Leadership
Building Unity	Intimacy
Agreement	Companionship
Nurture	Attractive Soul and Body
Defend	Listener

Spiritual Workout

Refuse to let anyone else meet these needs.

Look at your work and personal relationships and take an .honest look at whether you are allowing someone other than your spouse to meet one or more of these needs. If you are allowing someone to meet one of your deep relational needs other than your spouse, you are setting up the context of an affair and you need to quickly back out of the context, situations or even the relationship where this other person is meeting a need only your spouse should meet. If this continues you will eventually be drawn into an unhealthy even sexual relationship with this person. Look at the list below and see if you have crossed any professional or personal boundaries with someone.

Honor	Respect
Understanding	Adapt
Security	Domestic Leadership
Building Unity	Intimacy
Agreement	Companionship
Nurture	Attractive Soul and Body
Defend	Listener

Have you had an honest discussion with your spouse about your needs? Their needs?

chapter thirty-five

UNDERSTAND THE THREE ENEMIES OF THE CHRISTIANS

Understand how the three enemies of the Christian work against a God-honoring life : 1 John 2:15; Gal. 5:24; Rom. 6:11-13; Eph. 6:11-13

The Christian faces three enemies which want to promote immoral desires in his/her life to rob him/her from God's best. It is important that you understand what these three enemies are and how each of them works to try to cause lust to win. These are often referred to in a triplet form: The World, The Flesh, and the Devil. Each one strengthens destructive desires in different ways. Their ultimate aim is your defeat as an agent of God's grace and love in the world. They want to make you selfish and self-focused.

The World creates a value system and culture around you that emphasizes sensuality. It continually sends messages that giving in to desire is a good thing. It seeks to reinforce the idea that giving in to desire is the way to have your needs met. It does not want you to see the destruction that has come into the lives of those who embrace its value structure. The Apostle John says in 1 John 2:15, **"Do not love the world or the things in the world."** He means don't let its value structure and its answers begin to meet your needs. It is tempting to allow the world's answers to become our answers. But God has given us clear answers that really work and do not destroy our lives as we apply them. The world system has answers to all of our dilemmas also, but its answers always bring greater trauma. If you are lonely it says go have sex and you will forget that you are lonely. Yes, for a brief period you will forget, but you will have bigger problems after this short-term "solution." In every case where the world has an answer, it does not last very long and it brings with it problems that you never had before you tried its solution. The cultural messages that condones adultery and sexual expression outside of marriage are pathways to destruction. Do not accept the messages that swirl in the culture around you that temptation is an answer to your problems.

The second enemy that the Christian faces in its battle with sexual temptation is called in the Bible: The Flesh. This source of destructive desires is inside you. It is that principle of selfishness and sin that exists within you that you will not be free from until after you are with the Lord Jesus in heaven. The Flesh always puts your body's wants and desires ahead of anything else. It elevates what you want above God, above family, above your future, above your ultimate fulfillment, and above significance in life. It is a devastating enemy because it comes from within you. It will be a part of our earthly life until we go to be with Christ in heaven. The Flesh will harm, hurt, destroy, damage anyone or anything to get what it wants. Whenever you allow it to be in control you have put a selfish monster in charge of your life. It only knows how to push for what it wants. The Scripture is clear that you must not let it live in your life. You must crucify it on the cross that Christ died on. Gal. 5:24 **"Now those who belong to Christ Jesus have crucified the flesh with its passions and desires"** Rom. 6:11-13. **"Even so consider yourselves to be dead to sin, but alive to God in Christ Jesus. Therefore do not let sin reign in your mortal body so that you obey its lusts, and do not go on presenting the members of your body to sin as instruments of unrighteousness; but present yourselves to God as those alive from the dead, and your members as instruments of righteousness to God."** If you allow it to dictate what you do it will always pursue a selfish course, and destroy much of what you will need to build a meaningful life. Notice that this particular enemy you must crucify and/or play dead to its commands and assignments. The flesh is demanding to be obeyed quickly. This is why you need to immediately follow the promptings of the Holy Spirit to escape its pressure.

The third enemy of the Christian is the Devil. He is the source of the external assistants, tools and objects of lust. He wants you to give in to the flesh and be consumed in a selfish life. He does all he can to make it easy and convenient to sin. He is a master strategist seeking to move your particular desire within easy reach so that you will move past God's best for you and follow your fleshly desires. Listen to what the Apostle says about the work of the Devil in Eph. 6:11-13, **"Put on the full armor of God, so that you will be able to stand firm against the schemes of the devil. For our struggle is not against flesh and blood, but against the rulers, against the powers, against the world forces of this darkness, against the spiritual forces of wickedness in the heavenly places. Therefore, take up the full armor of God, so that you will be able to resist in the evil day, and having done everything, to stand firm."** Notice that the devil has schemes to get you to shame the Lord Jesus Christ. Do not fall for the convenient sin when it is clear that it is sin. It is the devil's provision. It cannot be God's will to commit adultery, or view pornography, or fill your mind with sexual fantasies. The devil is making it convenient, it is not God. In order to win against the wiles of the devil you must stand firm and resist. Do not take the convenient path of sin. Do the extra work to stay righteous even though it is difficult.

Many books and articles have been written on the power, work and plans of these three enemies. Realize that each of these wants you to destroy your life and rob you of God's best. Do not let them. Refuse to let the world's answers be your answers, no matter how many people tell you it's okay. Crucify your own selfish desires to get what you want now at all costs. Don't take the convenient path to sin.

Spiritual Workout

FITNESS

Which enemy are you currently facing the greatest pressure from (the world, the flesh, the devil) to give into sexual temptation? Please explain:

What is the world trying to get you to accept as moral and acceptable, but you know from Scripture it is not?

1.
2.
3.
4.
5.

What are 5 actions, thoughts or feelings in the last month that your flesh wanted you give in to? It can be very powerful to bring out into the open the pressure it is putting on you.

1.
2.
3.
4.
5.

What is the devil providing so that sexual sin is easy and convenient?

1.
2.
3.
4.
5.

CLOSE
SPIRITUAL
DOORWAYS

Close Spiritual Doorways Through Confession of Family, Cultural and National Sins: 1 John 1:9; Eph. 5:3-12; Dan. 9:3-20; Neh. 9:2, 3; Is. 6:1-6

Remember that there are three steps to *WINNING THE BATTLE*. Many times I have seen young men begin with energy and fervor to battle this powerful foe of lust. But they never quiet achieve a full victory because they have received temporary relief from the pressures of destructive desires through the initial exercises, and they did not push through to complete the war. Do not stop until you have worked through the whole Biblical battle plan against lust. This last step involves making sure that your family, nation, and culture does not leave you susceptible to greater levels of temptation in this area. In our day we have become largely ignorant to the spiritual connectedness of generations, nations, and cultures. But it is these insights that will help finish our victory in this battle with sin. We see the godly men of old closing spiritual doorways in this way so that they are freed up to pursue God with more vigor and purity.

chapter thirty-six

CLOSE NEGATIVE SPIRITUAL DOORWAYS BY CONFESSING FAMILY SINS

Close Negative Spiritual Doorways to You and Your Family:

Your parents, grandparents, and other ancestors have given you both a positive and a negative heritage. If their heritage included significant surrender in this area of sexual sin, then you will face a greater measure of temptation and attack to also give in to these sins. In order to be fully prepared and victorious over lust, sexual temptation, and destructive desires, you need to confess, renounce, repent, and spiritually cancel out the sins of your ancestors just like you have already done with your own. Realize that we live in a much more spiritually connected universe than our naturalistic worldview would suggest. This means that you will face increased temptation in the areas of sin that your ancestors repeatedly sinned in. Take the time to go back through the list of sexual sins mentioned at the beginning of this book, this time applying it to your family as a whole. Don't feel the need to dredge up the past by asking a lot of questions about your family's sins, but if you know that your family was involved in sexual sin, then it should be confessed, repented of and renounced. Obviously you did not commit these sins, but you can still acknowledge them before God as wrong. There is something powerful in agreeing with God about truth, sin, and allegiance. Confessing the sins of your forefathers, like Daniel and Nehemiah did, announces that you are standing with God. It has a strong cleansing action that washes away the filth and unrighteous connections that may attach to your family because of patterns of sin. This does not mean that you are disowning your family; you are bringing your family actions, habits and lifestyle into the light of God's truth. It is lining up with God's standard and letting the Lord and the angels know that you know right from wrong. When Jeremiah lamented over the city of Jerusalem and the fury that God unleashed against it, he was not shy in pointing out its sins. When Daniel was praying for his people, the people of God, he clearly declared that they had sinned against God, both individually and collectively, even though he, Daniel, had not sinned in those ways. When Isaiah was overcome by the vision of the Lord in the Temple, he confesses clearly that he is a man with unclean lips and the whole nation is also a people of foul and blasphemous mouths. When Nehemiah was governor of the city of Jerusalem he wanted to move the city forward, but he had to confront the past. But he confessed the sins of his ancestors and how reprehensible their sins were to God. He was seeing the same types of sin re-emerge in the people of Israel, and He wanted to cut them off from the past and start a new push for holy living.

Spiritual Workout

Make a list of your generational sins: Daniel 9; Nehemiah 9

Write the answers on another sheet of paper and then destroy the paper after you have confessed it to the Lord. We do not want to memorialize their sin, we want to confess it and open up a new level of freedom for Christ-like living.

Mother's Side	Father's side
1.	1.
2.	2.
3.	3.
4.	4.
5.	5.
6.	6.
7.	7.
8.	8.

Spiritual Workout:
Expanded Confession
of Sexual Sins

God describes each of the following as forms of sexual selfishness. Each of these sexual sins damages the individual; others, the society as a whole, and God's glory. Each is a twisting or distortion of God's design for sexual relations, and represents a level of selfishness that damages on a number of levels.

The question for this spiritual workout is whether any members of your family have given in to these levels of sexual sin. If they have, then just simply and clearly confess their involvement to the Lord as wrong and ask God for protection and cleansing from the impact of their sins.

Destructive Desire	Scripture	Definition
Zone 1:		**Sensuality**
Sensuality:	Gal. 5:19	Contemplation, conversation, jokes or viewing of sexually explicit material.
Lasciviousness:	Gal. 5:19	Actions, words, behaviors which are designed to stir up inside of yourself or others sexual ideas and actions which cannot be fulfilled within the context of marriage. This would include groping, indecent exposure, voyeurism, etc.
Mental Adultery:	Matt. 5:28	This is mental images and stories in which the individual participates in sexual practices with someone other than their spouse.
Transvestitism:	Deut. 22:5	This is where a person is trying to dress like a member of the opposite sex in order to stir up sexual desires within themselves or others.

Zone 2		Adultery
Premarital Adultery: Fornication:	Gal. 5:19; 1 Cor. 6:18	This is where a person has sexual relations with another person before their public commitment of marriage.
Adultery:	Matt. 5:27-30	This is when a person goes outside the boundaries of their marriage to engage in sexual intimacy with another person other than their spouse.
Prostitution:	1 Cor. 6:16-18	This is when a person (usually a man) pays a person to have sexual relations outside of the commitment of marriage.
Zone 3:		**Perversion or Distorted Sexuality:**
Homosexual Episodes:	Lev. 18:22; 20:13; Rom. 1:26, 27	This is where a person pursues sexual expression and climax with a person of the same sex. This is a perversion of the nature of sexual expression and context as designed by God.
Incest:		This is a perversion of sexual expression by having sexual expression and/or climax with one's own children.

Child Molestation:	Lev. 18:6-18; 20:14	This is a perversion of sexual expression by having sexual expression and/or climax with children under marriageable age.
Bestiality:	Lev. 18:23; 20:15,16	This is a selfish perversion of God's intended sexual expression by pursuing sexual expression or climax with and through animals.
Necrophilia:		This is a selfish perversion of God's intent for sexual expression by pursuing sexual expression and/or climax with the dead.
Incubus and Siccubus:	Gen. 6:4; Jude 1:6	This is a selfish perversion of God's intent for sexual expression by pursuing sexual expression, climax and/or procreation with spiritual beings.
Sacrificial Sexuality:	Lev. 18:21; 20:6; Deut. 19:14	This is a selfish perversion of God's intent for sexuality by pursuing sexual expression and climax through religious, occultic or satanic sexual rituals.

chapter thirty-seven

PICTURE THE EFFECTS OF LUST ON YOUR LOVED ONES

Picture the Effect of Lust on Those Connected to You:

Deut. 28:15-48; Exodus 34:7; Matt. 12:29

All sin committed by those in authority opens up the possibility of greater temptation for those under that person's care and leadership. The devil has to bind the strong man in order to get those in the strong man's charge. Matt 12:29 "Or how can anyone enter the strong man's house and carry off his property, unless he first **binds the strong man**? And then he will plunder his house." If you are a husband, parent, church leader, employer, or other type of leader, you have a responsibility to resist temptation, not just for your sake, but also for the sake of those who are under your leadership. Your giving into sin can wipe out the spiritual motivation and resistance to temptation of those under your care. Your lack of an outstanding moral example can be devastating to those who look up to you. Take time and examine what has happened to those under your care after you have given in to sexual temptation. Write out the difference(s) that you have seen or trouble they have seen and been drawn in to after you were conquered. We clearly see this kind of cascade of disaster when David gave in to sexual temptation to be with Bathsheba (2 Sam. 11-15).

One of the most potent weapons in our battle against lust is to picture what may happen to our children and loved ones if we continue to surrender to this temptation. Actually, mentally picture what may happen to your family, your wife, your career, your friends, or your finances if you continue to give in to lust. I have even had people pray to the Lord, "Could you give me a glimpse of the consequences if I keep giving in to sin in this area?" I believe the Lord wants us to be afraid of the consequences of sin which is why He spells out some of these consequences in Proverbs 1, 5 and 7 as well as the disastrous stories of Sampson, Lot, Jezebel, David, Eli and Samuel's sons, etc.

Spiritual Workout

Think through what could happen to the people in your life if you continue to give in to lust.

Spouse:

Children and Grandchildren:

Career:

Finances:

Friends:

Community:

Church:

Christ:

chapter thirty-eight

CLOSE EMOTIONAL DOORWAYS

Close Emotional Doorways

We open emotional doorways when we allow our feelings to continue to connect positively with sinful activity and sexual images and sexual relationships. Many times we have retained positive feelings about times of great sin which keeps those memories awake and alive in our minds. It is important to see our past times of sin through God's eyes, and no longer allow the short-term pleasure of sin to be the way we remember those events. Scripture is clear in Gal. 6:7, 8 **"Do not be deceived, God is not mocked; for whatever a man sows, this he will also reap. For the one who sows to his own flesh will from the flesh reap corruption, but the one who sows to the Spirit will from the Spirit reap eternal life."**

I remember working with a couple who said that they wanted to go deeper in their Christian life, but they seemed blocked at every turn. After much prayer and Scriptural assignments, I noticed some pictures in the hallway of their home. They seemed odd and unusually suggestive. I asked what these pictures were about and why they were hanging in the hallway of the home. They told me that the pictures were some of the happiest times of their lives. They had met a number of years before, going to parties where everyone got extremely loaded. While everyone was drunk and strung out, people had participated in all kinds of sexual sins and debauchery. During these times, someone had taken some pictures, and that was what hanging on the wall of their home. Each time they walked down the hallway they remembered back with fondness the happy times of sin. The wife actually remarked that she enjoyed her husband much more when he was drunk than since he sobered up. It was not until they took the symbols of their sin and rebellion against God off the walls of their home that they began to make new progress in their Christian life. They needed to confess that it was wrong to participate in these practices, and wrong to memorialize these events, and dangerous to attach such strong positive emotional feelings to begin to make progress in their Christian life. They had opened huge spiritual and emotional doorways for temptation and spiritual attack in their lives.

I am amazed at the number of people who have pictures, jewelry, trinkets and gifts that remind them of happy sinful times. No one else knows what they mean but they remain in the person's life keeping open the emotional doorway that sin is very pleasurable and enjoyable.

Spiritual Workout

Do you have strong positive emotional feelings attached to immoral actions?

> Debauched Parties:
>
> Sensual Friends:
>
> Adultery:
>
> Pornography:
>
> Other:

Spiritual Workout

Do you have pictures, jewelry, trinkets, gifts, etc. from past lovers, or friends that regularly remind you of happy sinful times? If you are going to really embrace a Christian mindset, then you must declare by your words and actions that sin is sin and destructive to a godly life.

Smash, burn, give back, throw away, or in some other way dispose of those mementos of sin. This will in many cases mark a significant break from the past as you push away at the pleasure that comes from sin and push forward to a life of holiness. Seek the Lord with a whole heart.

chapter thirty-nine

CLOSE PSYCHOLOGICAL DOORWAYS

Close Psychological Doorways.

We open sinful psychological doorways when refuse to see sexual activity the way that God sees it. Our culture has sought to approve sexual selfishness that God declares is harmful. Our culture is trying hard to move the boundaries of what is acceptable way past what God declares is His plan for a man and a woman. It is important to acknowledge God's moral boundaries as correct and righteous. We have lost the discipline of confessing truth and our agreement with that truth, but this ancient and powerful practice needs to be reintroduced.

Instead of trying to fit our problems, desires and selfishness into some form of normal, we need to weld ourselves to the truth and righteousness that is declared in Scripture. In this way we will be taking our thoughts captive to the Lord Jesus Christ in a new way. It is not enough to just say no to the designs and practices of lust. We must also clearly build fortresses of Godly truth that stand as places of refuge in our mind where we can find comfort, stability and protection from the slings and arrows of false thinking.

Do not leave open mental doorways by waffling on the legitimacy of aberrant expressions of sexuality. It is time to be clear about what you understand are righteous expressions of sexuality and what are not. Yes, various people because of their environment, upbringing and experiences do "feel" desires that are destructive to them. The fact that these desires come from within them does not make them right, or require that they live out those desires. It does not matter if this "feels" right to you or to them. If it is different from God's declared plan then it is wrong. God has given an objective standard. We must close this door. We must offer help and hope to those whose "feelings" and desires have been warped by their experiences, but we must not pretend that aberrant is normal.

Spiritual Workout

FITNESS

Agree with God in His design for marriage, sexuality and family. Agree with God that His perspective about sexual sin, temptation and boundaries is right. This is not in connection with any sin that you committed, it is just an announcement to yourself, to God and the angels that you agree with God's point of view.

Pray a prayer like this:

Dear Heavenly Father,

I come to You today in the name of the Lord Jesus Christ who died on a cross for my sins and bow in worship and surrender to You. I want to confess that You are right in what You approve and in what You disapprove. I completely agree with You, Heavenly Father, when You planned, designed and declared that mankind should enjoy the wonders of sexuality within the lifetime commitment of one man to one woman, called marriage. I agree with You that **SENSUALITY AND LASCIVIOUSNESS,** *as well as* **MENTAL ADULTERY,** *is wrong and against Your plan for the blessed life. Heavenly Father, I agree with You that* **CROSS-DRESSING AND PORNOGRAPHY** *are also wrong and not Your perfect design for sexual purity. I confess that You are right when You declare that* **FORNICATION, PROSTITUTION,** *and* **ADULTERY** *are outside of righteous boundaries. I also agree with Your condemnation of* **HOMOSEXUALITY, INCEST, BESTIALITY, DEMONIC SEXUALITY,** *and* **RITUALISTIC OCCULTIC SEXUALITY.** *I thank You, Heavenly Father, for being clear in Your Word as to the righteous way of expressing one's sexuality. I thank You for the wonder of marriage of one man and one woman, and its positive benefits for the individuals, the children and the society. I thank You, Lord Jesus, that You lived a perfect life and willingly surrendered that life to a horrible death on a cross as the perfect substitute for the sins of the whole world. I am thankful that You have provided a way out of the bondage of sin. Your plan for mankind's expression of sexuality within the boundaries of marriage is perfect. Your plan for rescuing those who have ignored and rebelled against that perfect plan is also perfect. Thank You for loving us with such a complete love.*

In the name of the Lord Jesus Christ, Amen.

chapter forty

CLOSE RELATIONAL DOORS

Closing Relational Doors:

Many people are involved in a dangerous game of keeping past relationships alive even though it could lead to sin in the future. The thrill of still being wanted or desired causes people to continue friendships that they should shut down. Invariably at a moment of weakness this relational doorway leads to adultery and destruction of so much.

Keeping old relationships that have a sensual undertone is foolish. I have watched too many times when old boyfriends stop by for a visit, and then in a few months it turns into an affair. This type of friendship is asking for trouble. I have watched as casual friendships that were started by volunteering for a sports season don't end when the activity ends. Then a few months later those friendships have led to adultery, and I am invited in to try to pick up the pieces of what they have destroyed. I have watched friendships develop at church through common interest in ministry that go past healthy discussions of ministry and become something more. Then a few months later I hear that the friendship became adulterous and there is wreckage everywhere. In our day and age it is important that we constantly be willing to evaluate our friendships and see if there are any that no longer need to be there.

Spiritual Workout

Do you have any opposite-sex friendships that you know you should shut down?

Do you have any same-sex friendships that you know you should shut down?

chapter forty-one

CLOSE NEGATIVE SPIRITUAL DOORWAYS BY CONFESSING NATIONAL SINS

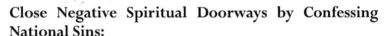

Close Negative Spiritual Doorways by Confessing National Sins:

Nations can become blind to sin and therefore make it easier for its citizens to violate God's law. All nations fall off of God's ideal in various directions and begin to condone the very thing that God says should be shameful and punished. Nations in various ways and at various stages condone harmful selfishness so that they can accomplish a certain goal or continue a particular benefit. After a while a nation stops noticing that the practice that they are allowing is harming their citizens. At this point it becomes imbedded into the national culture as permissible. Therefore there is no causal link made between this practice and the consequences that are bubbling up in the society. It is important for individuals to realize that they live in a culture that condones, in some ways, what God is against. Just as Daniel and Nehemiah recognized the sins of their nation, so we should recognize that our nation condones sensuality, adultery and even perversion in the name of liberty. Look at the Ten Commandments and act as a representative before God on behalf of your nation: where has your nation condoned the breaking of God's law? Even though you may not have broken God's commandment personally, if your nation as a whole sees nothing wrong with it, it is important to acknowledge your nation's spiritual blindness.

The Ten Commandments
God's definition of Love

Thou shall have no other gods before Me.

Thou shall not make for yourself any graven images.

Thou shall not take the name of the Lord your God in vain.

Remember the Sabbath Day to keep it holy.

Honor your father and your mother.

Thou shall not murder.

Thou shall not commit adultery.

Thou shall not steal.

Thou shall not bear false witness against your neighbor.

Thou shall not covet anything that belongs to your neighbor.

Lord, my nation/culture approves of _____ and yet You say it is wrong. I agree with You, Lord, that it is wrong and selfishly destructive. I want to publicly agree with You and Your standards for individuals, cultures and nations. I agree with You, Lord Jesus, that we are guilty before You as a nation/culture because of this. Please forgive us and draw many people to repentance and freedom through Your sacrifice for them.

In Jesus Christ name, Amen.

chapter forty-two

DEAL WITH HIDDEN WOUNDS

Deal With Hidden Wounds

One of the most common ways that spiritual, emotional, and psychological doorways remain open for future attack is to refuse to deal with wounds, hurts, bitterness and trauma of the past. This is especially true if the wound was sexual in nature. Many people just want to deny that anything ever happened. If you have a wound or deep hurt that you are unwilling to talk about or deal with, then lust can become the medication that you use to avoid dealing with the pain and difficulty. If the wound has been uncovered and is able to be discussed and viewed from a mature, unemotional point of view, then it no longer exerts its distorting influence in your life.

Now it is true that God gives children the ability to wall off certain memories that are too traumatic or painful until they are old enough to deal with these issues, feelings, and ideas. I am not advocating that children who have suffered abusive situations be made to face the pain, horror or brutalizing details of what happened to them. I am talking about adults who are unwilling to admit that something happened to them.

I have had the privilege of walking with a number of men and women through their spiritual journey to wholeness and healing. A significant part of many people's journey is uncovering old wounds and attacks. These wounds must be cleaned out and allowed to heal. Too often when a deep wound is sexual in nature it is covered, hidden and protected so that no one knows that it took place. This allows the trauma to become an infection spreading throughout the person's whole system. I have been a part of helping women who have been raped and brutalized by respected adults. It is when they bring out this pain and trauma into the light, that they begin to see this toxic factory of fear, doubt, self-loathing and shame begin to close down. I have helped men who have been betrayed sexually by coaches and friends, release the burden of that pain and move toward wholeness.

Dealing with wounds from the past is not an easy process. I wish that I could tell you that if you do these three steps then you will never have to deal with it again. It is much more complicated than that. But I can tell you that if you do not begin talking about this wound with trusted and helpful people, you will never begin moving toward wholeness.

Spiritual Workout:
Forgiveness

Have you been deeply wounded in the sexual arena by others in the past? If the answer is yes, please write down on a separate piece of paper, what took place to you, this is the first step toward your healing.

Who is a trusted friend or professional that you could talk with about the pain and wounds of the past?

Begin a process of appropriate blame, justice and/or punishment for those who have wronged you in the past.

Walk through a process of forgiveness so that the toxic effects of what they did to you will no longer poison your soul. It is helpful to find a trusted counselor or spiritual director to walk with your through this process of detailed application of Scripture so that you can release the individual to God in forgiveness.

CONCLUSION

Art was free. He had for years battled against sexual temptation that seemed to swamp him and lead him to disastrous actions that threatened to end his marriage, his career and his reputation. But now he was working this program of spiritual exercises that allowed him to turn away from the seduction of lust. He did not think it could be done when he started. "I did not believe that it was possible," he told me after 6 months of working with this program. "As long as I keep up with the spiritual exercises, especially the meditation on Scripture, I win and my family wins." There is so much more power in doing the Word of God than he ever thought or had experienced before. Art was now beginning to show the potential that everyone knew that he possessed, but had never really shown. He was taking the lead in his marriage. He was up for promotions and tackling new assignments at work. He was willing to step forward at church and use his knowledge, skills and experience. There was a whole new health coming to the family because Dad was no longer off somewhere else, he was engaged with the kids. He had been, for years, held back by the chains of shame, guilt, lust and secrecy. They were not holding him back anymore. It is this writer's desire that after reading and beginning to practice some of the exercises in this book, you are experiencing the freedom and power of living above the bondage of sexual temptation. Please realize that just reading this book will not result in any change in your battle with temptation, you must begin practicing the exercises that are detailed in this manual. You are looking for the 10 exercises that are your secret weapons that will always allow you to win. It is the doing of Scripture that releases the power of God in a person's life (Luke 6:46, James 1:22)

This book is about three steps that are essential to overcome destructive desires. **First,** cleanse your life through confession of past sexual sins. **Second,** prepare fully for sexual temptation and desires. **Third,** close spiritual, mental, emotional and relational doorways. Each of these three steps needs to be repeated over and over with different spiritual exercises in order gain the victory in this battle with lust.

In order to win the battle against destructive desires, you must take advantage of the direction, power and provision that God has given in His word. It is not enough to know what the Word says if you are not actually working it out in some form in your life. You have to get serious about battling and winning against lust. Realize what is at stake if you give in to lust, and what there is to gain by putting other people ahead of your selfish sexual urges.

You cannot win this battle alone. There are many weapons that are available for your individual use. But there are also some Biblical weapons that are group exercises. Too often we have tended to isolate and try to solve all of our problems by ourselves. One of the best ways to make progress and grow to being a truly blessed and loving person is to get involved with a group of men who are interested in being honest with each other. Get into a small group at your church. Start a small group of like minded men at work.

I believe that every church needs to have an ongoing ministry of actually working with men to get a handle on their battle with sexual temptation and addiction. It cannot be just a one-time class for a few weeks. This needs to be a constantly repeated discipleship program. Men can take the class, learn about these various projects, practice on Biblical applications, and learn how to live above the world systems pulling toward sensuality. They can take the class once a year. They can take it every few years. If they have a deep seated battle with lust, then they can just stay in the class for a year or two until they begin to consistently win. We need Christian men to begin to win in this battle with lust. Men need to know that there is a solution to this problem. Men's groups and Counseling centers, as well as churches, can use this material to form the basis of help to men who are struggling with this problem.

One of the great dangers is that a person will read the material in this book and say, "Yes that material will definitely work in the battle against self-destruction, but I don't have time, or I don't know if I want to go to all that trouble. You must actually do the exercises or the book will do you no good.

APPENDIX #1

This handout is designed to allow you to review any sexual sins that you have been involved in, and then destroy it so that no one but God and you know what you confessed. It can be helpful during your time of confession to indicate in some way your involvement in these sins. This could be through making dots on the page next to what you have done. It could be with writing initials or dates or one word descriptors. The idea is to really acknowledge that you have violated God's standards and are seeking His forgiveness that comes through Jesus Christ. If you are using this book as a class or small group, please feel free to copy these two pages out of the book and use as a handout that people can work through, and then tear up, burn or discard in some permanent way.

Destructive Desire	Scripture	Definition
Zone 1:		**Sensuality**
Sensuality:	Gal. 5:19	Contemplation, conversation, jokes or viewing of sexually explicit material.
Lasciviousness:	Gal. 5:19	Actions, words, behaviors designed to stir up inside of yourself or others sexual ideas and actions which cannot be fulfilled within the context of marriage. This would include groping, indecent exposure, voyeurism, etc.
Mental Adultery:	Matt. 5:28	Mental images and stories and fantasies in which the individual participates in sexual practices with someone other than their spouse.
Transvestitism:	Deut. 22:5	This is where a person is trying to dress like a member of the opposite sex in order to stir up sexual desires within themselves or others.

Zone 2		Adultery
Fornication:	Gal. 5:19; 1 Cor. 6:18	This is when a person has sexual relations with another person before their public commitment of marriage.
Adultery:	Matt. 5:27-30	This is when a person goes outside the boundaries of their marriage to engage in sexual intimacy with another person other than their spouse.
Prostitution:	1 Cor. 6:16-18	This is when a person (usually a man) pays a person to have sexual relations outside of the commitment of marriage.

Zone 3:		Perversion /Distorted Sexuality:
Homosexual Episodes:	Lev. 18:22; 20:13; Rom. 1:26, 27	This is where a person pursues sexual expression and climax with a person of the same sex. This is a perversion of the nature of sexual expression and context as designed by God.
Incest:	Lev. 17:6-18	This is a perversion of sexual expression by having sexual expression and/or climax with one's family members or relatives.
Child Molestation:	Lev. 18:6-18; 20:14	This is a perversion of sexual expression by having sexual expression and/or climax with children under marriageable age.
Bestiality:	Lev. 18:23; 20:15,16	This is a selfish perversion of God's intended sexual expression by pursuing sexual expression or climax with and through animals.
Necrophilia:		This is a selfish perversion of God's intent for sexual expression by pursuing sexual expression and/or climax with the dead.
Incubus and/or Siccubus:	Gen. 6:4; Jude 1:6	This is a selfish perversion of God's intent for sexual expression by pursuing sexual expression, climax and/or procreation with spiritual beings.
Sacrificial Sexuality:	Lev. 18:21; 20:6; Deut. 19:14	This is a selfish perversion of God's intent for sexuality by pursuing sexual expression and climax through religious, occultic or satanic sexual rituals.

APPENDIX #2

Prayer of Confession for Zone 3 Sexual Sins

Confession and Repentance: 1 John 1:9; 2 Tim. 2:24
Lord Jesus, I agree with You that _____ is wrong. I turn away from it and ask that all the forgiveness that is in your death on Calvary be applied to my sin in this area. You say in Your Word that _____ is wrong. I realize that only in Your power and energy and through Your direction can I successfully turn away from this sin.

Renunciation: 2 Cor. 4:4
I repudiate, reject and renounce any ground, place or power I gave to Satan in my life through my involvement in _____ _____. I give to the Lord Jesus Christ all power over this area of my life. I willingly surrender this area to the Lord Jesus Christ and the Holy Spirit.

Cleansing and Expulsion: 1 John 1:9; Eph. 4:27
I cancel out any contract I may have made with Satan through _____. I ask You, Lord Jesus, to cleanse me of any and all unrighteousness (mental, emotional, physical and spiritual) in answer to Your promise to cleanse me from all unrighteousness if I would confess them to You.

Transfer of Ownership and Infusion of the Spirit of Truth: 2 Cor. 10:3-5; Col. 3:1:27, 28; Eph. 5:18
I, right now, transfer ownership of sexuality and relationships in my life to the Lord Jesus. I choose to take every thought regarding sex, lust and sexual pleasure captive to Christ (2 Cor. 10:3-5) and

allow Him full Lordship in this area. I ask You, Lord Jesus, that You would fill this area of my life with the Holy Spirit of Truth, so that I would be wise, thankful and able to see Your plan in this area in the future. Thank You, Lord Jesus, for dying on the Cross for me. I choose to cooperate with You in the sexual area of my life so that the process You began in me when I first trusted in You can be completed (Phil 1;6). I realize that You want to display through me the character qualities of the Lord Jesus (Col. 1:27,28; Gal. 2:20).

In the name and for the glory of the Lord Jesus Christ, Amen.

In order for this prayer of confession to be maximally effective in breaking very strong sexual strongholds and influence, it is best if this prayer is prayed aloud with a mature Christian brother or prayer team present who is praying with and for you.

APPENDIX #3

The Armor of God: The Breastplate of Truth

Bible	Inspired, Inerrant, Objective communication from beyond our Universe	He has given us the way to beat these enemies and an inerrant game plan for life: Righteous living.
God	Essence: Infinite, Self-existent, Spirit Attributes: Omnipotent, Omnipresence, Omniscience, Immutable, Holy, Good, True, Sovereign, Righteous Nature: Triune: Father, Son and Holy Spirit. Names: Almighty, Creator, Father, I AM, Provider.	He sees what you are doing. He knows what you are planning. He has not changed His mind on sexual sin. He above and beyond any conception of God. He is pure and untainted by sin. He is in an eternal sustaining loving relationship.
Jesus	God of God, Son of God, Creator, Savior, Lord, Judge of all the earth, Intercessor for believers, Advocate, Alpha and Omega.	He loves me and wants me to live above selfishness.
Holy Spirit	God of God, Third person of the Tri-unity of God, Sealer, Regenerator, Convictor, Guide.	Holy Spirit is guiding me and is grieved when I get selfish.
Salvation	Provided by God, gracious gift of forgiveness and righteousness before God, dynamic energy to live holy lives, resurrected body, intimate knowledge of God, glorification, heaven.	God has forgiven me through Christ. He has given me new power and truth to win in this area.
Man; Angels	Fallen image-bearer of God; Material and Immaterial being There are other intelligent spirit beings that occupy God's universe. Some who are righteous and some who are wicked.	God made man body, soul and spirit. I cannot let the body dominate the soul or the spirit. Evil angelic beings study people and plot to tempt them with sexual desire.

Church	Creation of God, designed to worship, disciple, evangelize, fellowship and compassion.	God designed the church to support each other because we can't do it alone. Are you trying to be a Lone Ranger?
Return of Christ	Imminent and Personal return of Christ, The King will return to claim the earth.	Christ will return. Do you want Him to come back while you are giving in to sexual temptation?
Heaven; Hell; Judgment Day	In the presence of God enjoying interaction with God, enjoying perfect service for Him. Away from the presence of God, except for wrath. Evaluation of every thought, word, deed, attitude and motive in our whole life.	God offers us heaven, act like you are going there. There is a place of separation from the grace and mercy of God. God is watching everything you say, do, think. He wants to reward Christians for their actions that line up with His will.

APPENDIX #4

The Armor of God

The Armor of God	Verses	Application
Stand Firm	Eph. 6:14 Put on the full armor of God, so that you will be able to stand firm against the schemes of the devil... Stand firm, therefore.	Practice taking no action, either mentally or physically toward sin. If a sensual picture is available for viewing, you take no action to look at it. . . . If a woman is flirting or being suggestive in some fashion, you do not return the flirting, you do not act in any way interested, you do not touch, or in any way signal with your eyes, face, mouth, hands or body that you are interested.
Christian Truth	Eph. 6:14 Having girded your loins with truth	Remind yourself again of the truth of the Christian worldview. The ultimate reality in the universe is the Triune God. Above, beyond and before anything, there is a Supreme Being we know of as God. He created the universe out of nothing, separate from Himself. He loved us enough to send His Son to pay the penalty for our selfishness and sin. He has communicated with us clearly and objectively without error in the Scriptures. He guides the Christian with His Holy Spirit. We can be forgiven of our sins and selfishness and have right relationship with God through belief in Jesus Christ's life and death. Jesus Christ died, was buried and rose from the dead. Mankind was created by God in His image but now is corrupted with a natural inclination

		toward selfishness and sin. God has called each Christian to join with other Christians to worship Him, to grow in understanding and Christian living, to evangelize others, to deeply connect with others, to help the poor and afflicted. There is an after-life where heaven and/or hell will be the final real destination of individuals. History will have an end when Jesus Christ returns a second time and breaks into human history as ruler and King.
Righteousness	Eph. 6:14 Having put on the Breastplate of Righteousness,	Give thanks for the perfect life and death of Christ that allows God to establish a loving, accepting relationship with you. Eliminate anything you are doing that is clearly not righteous or pleasing to the Lord. Look for opportunities to meet the needs of others or benefit them in some way.
Peace	Eph. 6:15 and having shod your feet with the Preparation of the Gospel of Peace;	Re-embrace your acceptance of your absolute need of Christ's perfect life, death and resurrection. It is Christ's work that has allowed you to be at peace with God and nothing can separate you from His loving relationship with you. Remind yourself that your relationship with God does not depend on you but on what Christ has already done. Because of all that God through Christ has forgiven you of... stop fighting, hating, criticizing those who hurt, wound or slander you.
Salvation	Eph. 6:16 In addition to all, taking up the shield of faith with which you will be able to extinguish all the flaming arrows of the evil one.	Force your mind to think again of what Christ has won for you through His life, death and resurrection. God chose you, before the world began, to receive His love and be in His family. You can relate to God directly because of the forgiveness of your sins. You are a member of God's forever family. God is working within you to make you more Christ-like. You have a

		home and citizenship in heaven. You are saved from facing the wrath of God. Christ is coming back for you. Heaven is where the life will be revealed of which we only catch glimpses. You have been given a guide for this life's path called the Holy Spirit. You find joy in purity instead of impurity. You have been forgiven. You will be given rewards for every Christ-like action you perform. You have God's love flowing through you.
Faith	Eph. 6:17 And take the Helmet of Salvation,	Commit again to trusting God's guidance, plans, lifestyle, and wisdom for your life. His way of life is a superior way of life for you. He is still in control. He can stop this difficult period whenever He wants. He loves you and will show you the way of escape. It is worthwhile to live God's way and trust Him.
Scripture	Eph 6:17 And the Sword of the Spirit, which is the Word of God.	Recite particular Scripture over and over again, under your breath, in your head or out-loud. Verses like Ps. 119:9-11; 1 Thess. 4:3-5; 2 Tim. 2:22. Make little cards with these and other powerful Scriptures on them that you can carry with you all the time to refer to and read out loud when you face these times.
Prayer	Eph. 6:18 With all prayer and petition pray at all times in the Spirit, and with this in view, be on the alert with all perseverance and petition for all the saints...	Ask God for strength to do the righteous thing instead of the sensual or selfish thing. Ask God to empower, bless, direct, and rebuke every person you know until the power of the temptation has passed. Keep praying for others until the power of the temptation is lessened and you can move on to other things.

APPENDIX #5

This is a reduced copy of the material on the Fear of the Lord so that you can make a copy and carry it with you.

5 Aspects of the Fear of the Lord	Verses:
1) The desire to please and reverence God with our actions.	Prov. 2:5 Then you will discern the **fear of the Lord** and discover the knowledge of God.
2) The desire to receive the blessings that God gives to follow His commands.	James 1:17 Every good thing given and every perfect gift is from above, coming down from the Father of lights, with whom there is no variation or shifting shadow. Prov. 15:16 "Better is a little with the **fear of the Lord** than great treasure and turmoil with it."
3) The realization that there is coming a Judgment Day.	2 Cor. 5:10,11 For we must all appear before the judgment seat of Christ, so that each one may be recompensed for his deeds in the body, according to what he has done, whether good or bad. Therefore, knowing the fear of the Lord, we persuade men, but we are made manifest to God.
4) Embracing the truth that everything we have ever said and done will be evaluated and seemingly shown to others who may need or want to know.	Luke 12:2 But there is nothing covered up that will not be revealed, and **hidden** that will not be known.
5) God has set up consequences for when we disobey His design for righteous living.	Gal. 6:7 Do not be deceived, God is not mocked; for whatever a man sows, this he will also reap. Prov. 8:13 The **fear of the Lord** is to hate evil; Pride and arrogance and the evil way And the perverted mouth, I hate.

BIBLIOGRAPHY

Every Man's Battle: Steve Arteburn., Waterbook Press, 2374 Telstar Dr. Suite 160, Colorado Springs, Colorado 80920.

New American Standard Bible, Lockman Foundation, 1995.

The Drug of the New Millennium: The Science of How Internet Pornography Radically Alters the Human Brain and Body. Mark Kastleman, Content Watch Articles.

Becoming a Godly Husband: The Hardest Thing a Man Will Ever Do Is Really Love His Wife, Gil Stieglitz, Wine Press Publications, Enumclaw, Washington, 2000.

Becoming a Godly Wife, Gil Stieglitz, Pathway Press, Cleveland, Tenn. 2006.

Spiritual Disciplines of a C.H.R.I.S.T.I.A.N., Gil Stieglitz., Wine Press Publications, Enumclaw, Washington. 2005.

The Living Bible, Ken Taylor.

WEBSITES:

Center for Disease Control Web site:
US Government site for Women:
Content watch: *www.contentwatch.org*
Kidsbiz: *www.kidsbiz.org*

OTHER RESOURCES BY GIL STIEGLITZ

BOOKS
Spiritual Disciplines of C.H.R.I.S.T.I.A.N.
Becoming a Godly Husband
Becoming a Godly Wife (Co-authored with Dana Stieglitz)
Winning the Battle over Temptation
Breaking Satanic Bondage
Developing Godly Leaders
Keeping Visitors
Snapshots in the Life of Jesus

VIDEOS
Growing a Vibrant and Healthy Church
Relationships Conference: There are only 5 Problems in Marriage
Spiritual Disciplines of a C.H.R.I.S.T.I.A.N. (Master's Level Series)
Preaching: A Problem Solutions Approach

AUDIO
Ten Commandments
God's Principles for Handling Money
4 Essential of Great Parenting
How to be a Winner with People

WEB PAGE
Please visit Principles to Live By on the web:*www.ptlb.com*. This is a non profit ministry committed to providing practical Biblical material to educate the world on how to live out God's principles. Please visit the site and check out all the materials.